FELTED BAGS

FELTED BAGS

30 ORIGINAL BAG DESIGNS TO KNIT AND FELT

ALICE UNDERWOOD & SUE PARKER

GUILD OF MASTER
CRAFTSMAN PUBLICATIONS

First published 2009 by

Guild of Master Craftsman Publications Ltd.
Castle Place, 166 High Street, Lewes,
East Sussex BN7 1XU

ISBN 978-1-86108-654-9

A catalogue record for this book is available from the
British Library.
Associate Publisher Jonathan Bailey
Production Manager Jim Bulley
Managing Editor Gerrie Purcell
Senior Project Editor Dominique Page
Editor Alison Howard
Managing Art Editor Gilda Pacitti
Design Simon Goggin and Chloë Alexander

Set in Helvetica Neue
Colour origination by GMC Reprographics
Printed and bound in China by Hing Yip Printing Co. Ltd.

Picture credits
Styled photographs of the bags by Laurel Guilfoyle.
All other photographs of the bags by Anthony Bailey,
GMC Publications.

Other photographs as follows:
Alice Underwood: 35, 39, 41, 45, 49, 61, 81, 97,
98, 120.
Chloë Alexander: 127.
Flickr.com: 9 OakleyOriiginals; 23 Adorenomis;
29 Ivan Mlinaric; 56 jennifrog; 57 ShashiBellamkonda;
65 jonathanb1989; 69 Jim Linwood; 70 wauter de
tuinkabouter; 74 Gato Azul; 77 icelight; 89 Gaetan Lee;
93 geishaboy500; 105 missteee; 119 rallycarter;
123 Randy, Son of Robert; 131 alvanman; 132 andyket.
iStockphoto.com: 115.
James Underwood: 19, 21, 83, 85, 109.
John R Lane: 51.
Nick Lovick: 13.
Rebecca Mothersole: 139.
stock.xchng.com: 52 andrebog.

FOREWORD

Anyone who does the laundry is likely to have had the unfortunate experience of felting a much-loved jumper by mistake. Washing an untreated wool garment in a washing machine or vigorously rubbing a delicate alpaca cardigan in hot water will result in felt, making them for ever unwearable. In our book, this quality of wool is put to good use, intentionally turning loose knitting into sturdy felt in your washing machine.

Felting is the result of the fact that animal hair is coated in scales like those of a fish or fir cone. In the washing machine the scales are scuffed up by the heat, wetness and agitation and so they lock together into a dense fabric. The ease with which this happens depends on the animal (sheep, goat, alpaca) and sometimes on the individual breed.

Crafters who make wet felt from combed wool tops will know what a labour of love and sweat (and possibly tears) this can be. The method of knitting then felting, as presented in this book, offers the chance to felt without the need to get your hands wet!

Our bags have been inspired by textiles, architecture, nature and life events. We have included designs that are suitable for beginners, and more advanced ones for those who enjoy a challenge. Some of the techniques that are required may be new to you, so you will find these explained at the back of the book. Yarns from all over the world have been used, including some from rare breeds of sheep; a list of suppliers is also provided at the back.

It has been fantastic fun and a huge learning experience for us to write this, our first book. We hope you have as much fun knitting the designs.

A word of warning
If you choose to substitute your own choice of wool to make the design your own, please, please, please test it out first to avoid disappointment with the finished item.

Alice Underwood and **Sue Parker**

CONTENTS

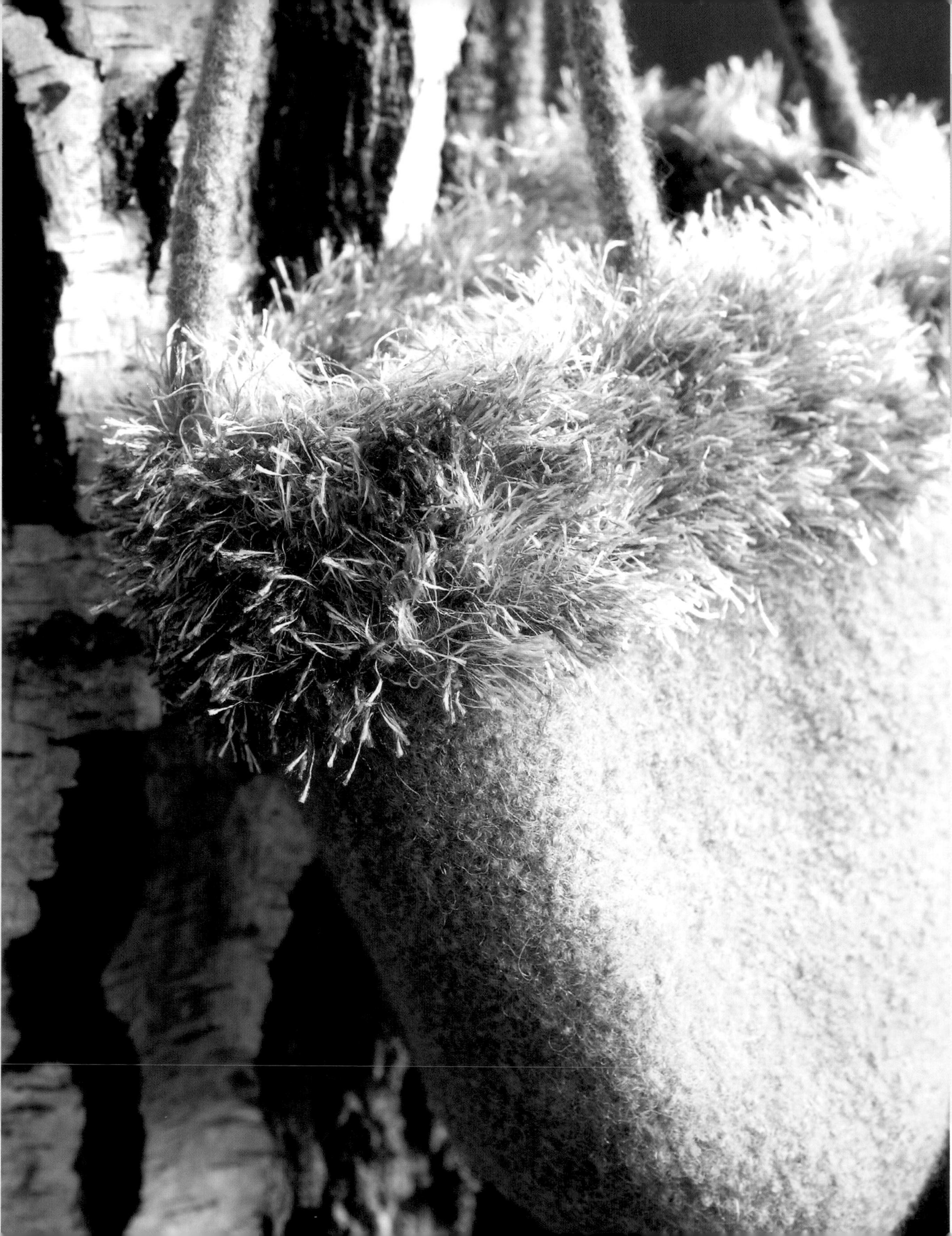

ICY GRASS

One of the first signs of winter is waking to discover that the grass has turned white overnight. The long blades hang down under the weight of the ice, each taking on a unique form. This natural phenomenon can be echoed by felting with an eyelash yarn, and is used to great effect round the top of this bag.

COLOURS INCORPORATED

MATERIALS

❖ *(250g) aran-weight pure wool*

❖ *50g Wendy Cosmic polyester eyelash yarn*

❖ *A pair of 5.5mm straight needles (US9:UK5)*

❖ *A 5.5mm circular needle (US9:UK5)*

❖ *A pair of 4.5mm double-pointed needles (US7:UK7)*

❖ *4 stitch markers*

❖ *3 stitch holders or safety pins*

❖ *Wool needle to graft handles and finish off ends of yarn*

❖ *Magnetic clasp (optional)*

Note: do not use superwash or machine-washable wool, and use the stated eyelash yarn if possible, as different brands vary greatly.

DIMENSIONS

BEFORE FELTING

Base **W** 13½in (34cm) Base **D** 4¾in (12cm)

Bag **H** 14½in (36.5cm)

❖

AFTER FELTING

Base **W** 9½in (24cm) Base **D** 4in (10.5cm)

Bag **H** 8½in (22cm)

DIFFICULTY RATING ✪ ✪

SPECIAL TECHNIQUES

Garter stitch *see page 145*
Stocking stitch *see page 145*
Using stitch markers *see page 147*

Working in the round *see pages 148–9*
Making an I-cord *see page 150*
Grafting stitches *see page 151*

Felting *see page 152*
Attaching a magnetic clasp *see page 155*

INSTRUCTIONS

This bag is worked in the round using a circular needle.

The base

Using 5.5mm straight needles, cast on 48 sts and knit 34 rows in garter stitch. Change to the circular needle and knit across the sts on the straight needle. Pick up and knit 22 sts along the short edge of the base, 48 sts along the second long edge and 22 sts along the second short edge, placing a stitch marker at each corner (140 sts).

The sides

Knit 60 rounds, moving the markers across as they are reached. At this point the bag will be approximately 11¾in (30cm) high. Join in eyelash yarn and, using both yarns together, decrease on the next round to compensate for the fact that the eyelash yarn will shrink less as follows:

Decrease row: K1, (k2tog, k2) 34 times, k2tog, k1 (105 sts).
Note: where a marker falls between two stitches that are knitted together, move forward 1 stitch.

Next round: Knit to the last 2 sts, k2tog (104 sts).
Note: at this point the markers should indicate two long sides of 36 sts each and two short sides of 16 sts each.

Knit 12 more rounds without decreasing, ending at the marker at the start of the round.

The handles

Next round: Using pure wool only, k7. Cast off 22 sts. *K4, place the 5 sts from the needle on a stitch holder or safety pin**. Cast off 20 sts. Work * to ** once more. Cast off 22 sts. Work * to ** once. Cast off 20 sts. Knit to end (5 sts remain on the needle).
Note: there should now be a total of four sets of 5 sts to form the handles.

Making up

Transfer the 5 remaining sts to a double-pointed needle and, using pure wool, work in I-cord for 31½in (80cm). Graft these sts to the 5 sts remaining on the same long side of the bag. Repeat to make an identical handle on the other side. Finish off all ends of yarn by weaving into the work before felting.

FELTING

Felt the bag in the washing machine, ensuring that the maximum temperature does not exceed 140°F (60°C), to protect the polyester eyelash yarn. Our examples felted sufficiently with two 140°F (60°C) washes.

Attaching a clasp (optional)

Fasten a magnetic clasp to either side of the inside upper edge of the bag if desired.

VARIATION
Colours incorporated

11

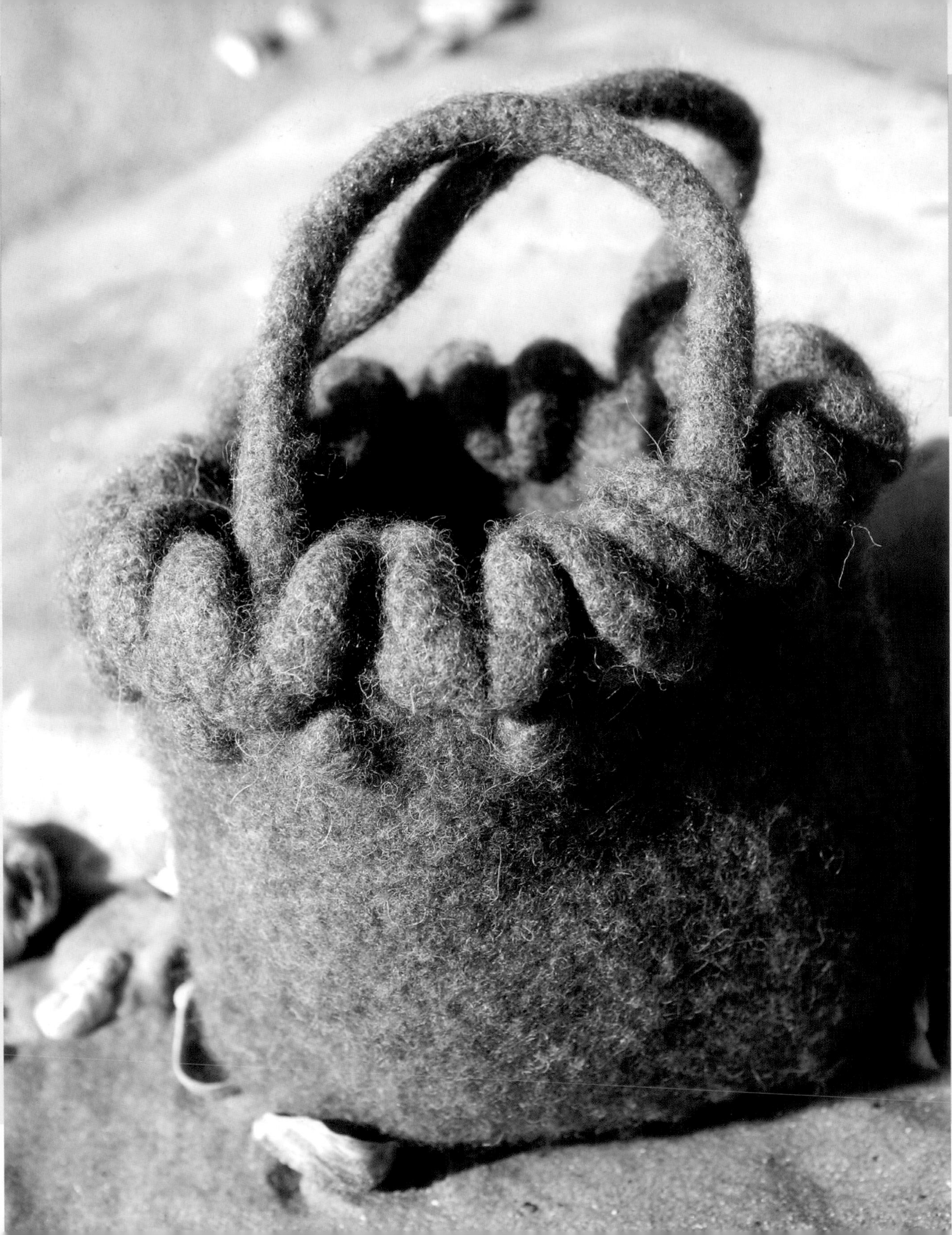

RONALDSAY BEACH

This design was inspired by the rocky shoreline and the stormy waters of North Ronaldsay in the Orkneys. The island's sheep are a primitive British breed with an interesting history. In 1832, the inhabitants built a wall right round North Ronaldsay to protect their grazing land. Banished to the shoreline outside the wall, the sheep adapted to survive mainly on seaweed.

COLOURS INCORPORATED

MATERIALS

- ❖ *150g aran-weight pure wool*
- ❖ *A pair of 5.5mm straight needles (US9:UK5)*
- ❖ *A 5.5mm circular needle (US9:UK5)*
- ❖ *A pair of 4.5mm double-pointed needles (US7:UK7)*
- ❖ *4 stitch markers*
- ❖ *Wool needle to finish off ends of yarn*

Note: our main bag was made using British Breeds Manx Loghtan wool, the variation using Sheepfold's North Ronaldsay wool.

DIMENSIONS

BEFORE FELTING
Base **W** 6¼in (16cm) Base **D** 3¼in (8.5cm)
Bag **H** 9½in (24cm)

AFTER FELTING
Base **W** 5½in (14cm) Base **D** 3in (8cm)
Bag **H** 6¾in (17cm)

DIFFICULTY RATING ✛ ✛ ✛

Chart for Ronaldsay Beach

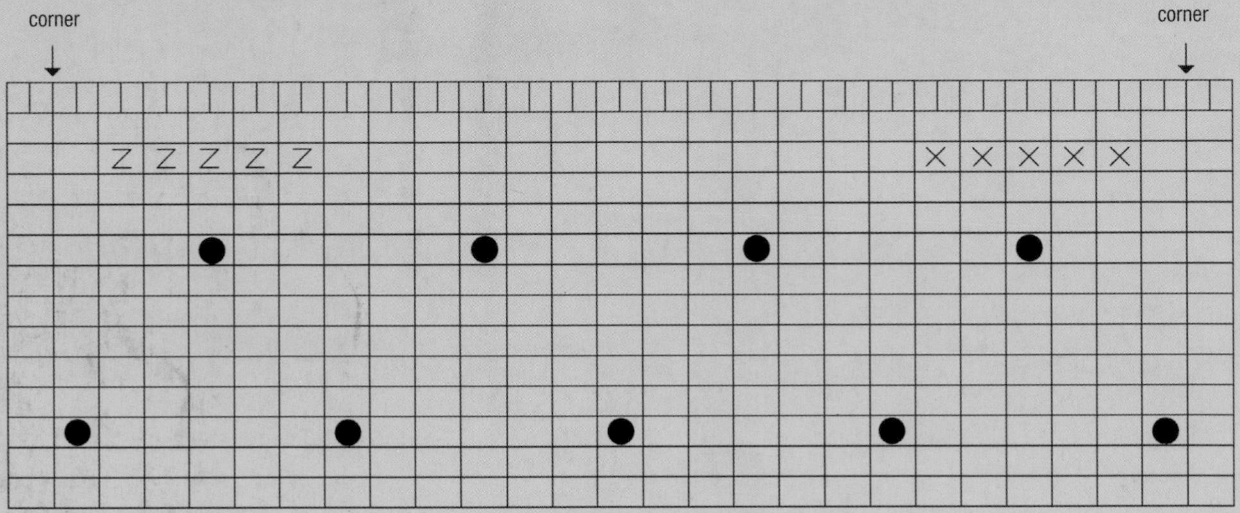

corner

corner

Key

Knit 1 stitch

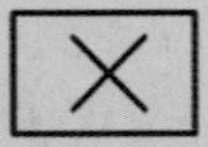

Pick up and knit 1 st, on the inside of the bag

Bobble

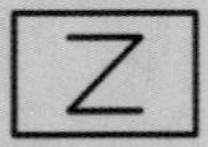

Attach the cast-off I-cord to these stitches, on the inside of the bag

SPECIAL TECHNIQUES
Garter stitch *see page 145*
Stocking stitch *see page 145*
Using stitch markers *see page 147*
Working in the round *see pages 148–9*
Making an I-cord *see page 150*
Felting *see page 152*
Making a bobble *instructions below*
Frill *instructions below*

INSTRUCTIONS

This bag is worked in rounds using a circular needle.

The base

Using the 5.5mm straight needles, cast on 25 sts and knit 22 rows in garter stitch. Change to the circular needle and knit across the sts from the straight needle. Pick up and knit 11 sts along the short edge of the base, 25 sts along the second long edge and 11 sts along the second short edge, placing a stitch marker at each corner (72 sts).

The sides

Knit 38 rounds, moving the markers across as they are reached, ending at the marker at the start of the round. At this point the bag will be approximately 7–8in (18–20cm) high. Now work the bobble and frill design described, and shown in the chart on page 14.

ABBREVIATIONS

mB: *K1, p1, k1, p1, k1, p1 all in the first stitch. Turn work, k6 loosely. Turn, purl first 3 sts tog, purl next 3 sts tog, pass the first stitch over the second and off the needle, leaving a single stitch to complete the bobble.*

m1: *Make one stitch by picking up the loop lying between the last and the next stitch and knitting into the back of it.*

The bobble design

First bobble round: *mB, k5**. Repeat * to ** the end of the round, so the first stitch in each set of 6 is the bobble (12 bobbles, each 5 sts apart).
Knit 5 rounds.

Second bobble round: K3, repeat * to ** 11 times, mB, k2. You will again have worked 12 bobbles, each 5 sts apart, with each bobble sitting half way between the bobbles on the preceding bobble round.
Knit 4 rounds.

The frill design

Round 1: *K1, m1**. Repeat * to ** to the end of the round (144 sts).
Round 2: Repeat round 1 (288 sts).
These two rounds are tight to knit, but persevere.

Knit 1 round then cast off all stitches, k-wise.

The handles

With wrong side facing and using a double-pointed needle, pick up and knit the 5 sts above the bobble just before the start of the frill (see chart). Work in I-cord for 13¾in (35cm). Join to the sts above the bobble at the other end of the same long side of the bag (see chart). Repeat for the handle on the other side.

Making up

Finish off all ends of yarn by weaving into the work before felting.

FELTING

Felt the bag in the washing machine. Before each wash, make sure the bobbles sit firmly on the outside of the bag to maximize the effect. You may need to pull each one firmly into place after each wash. Our examples felted sufficiently with two 140°F (60°C) washes.

VARIATION
Colours incorporated

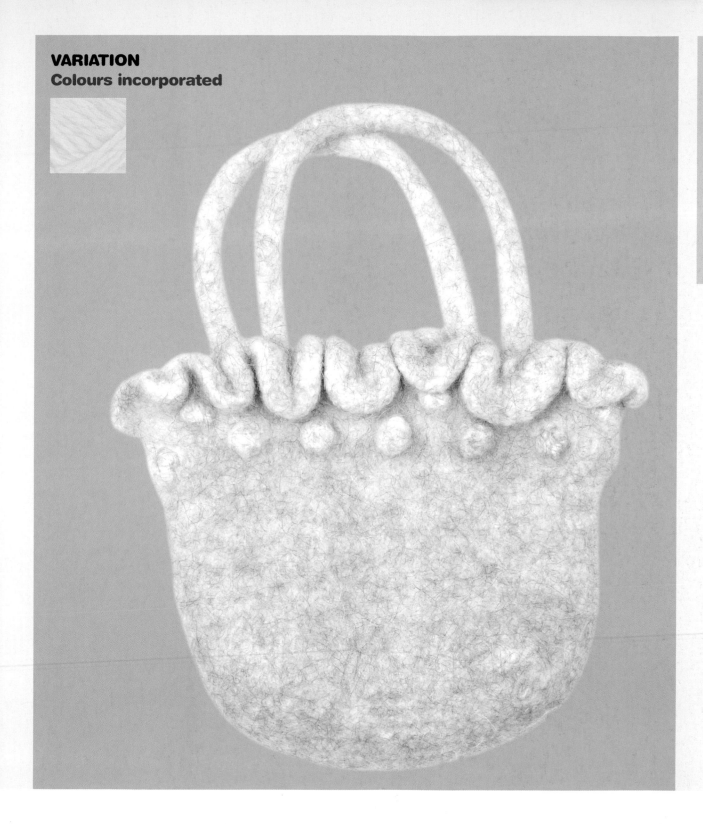

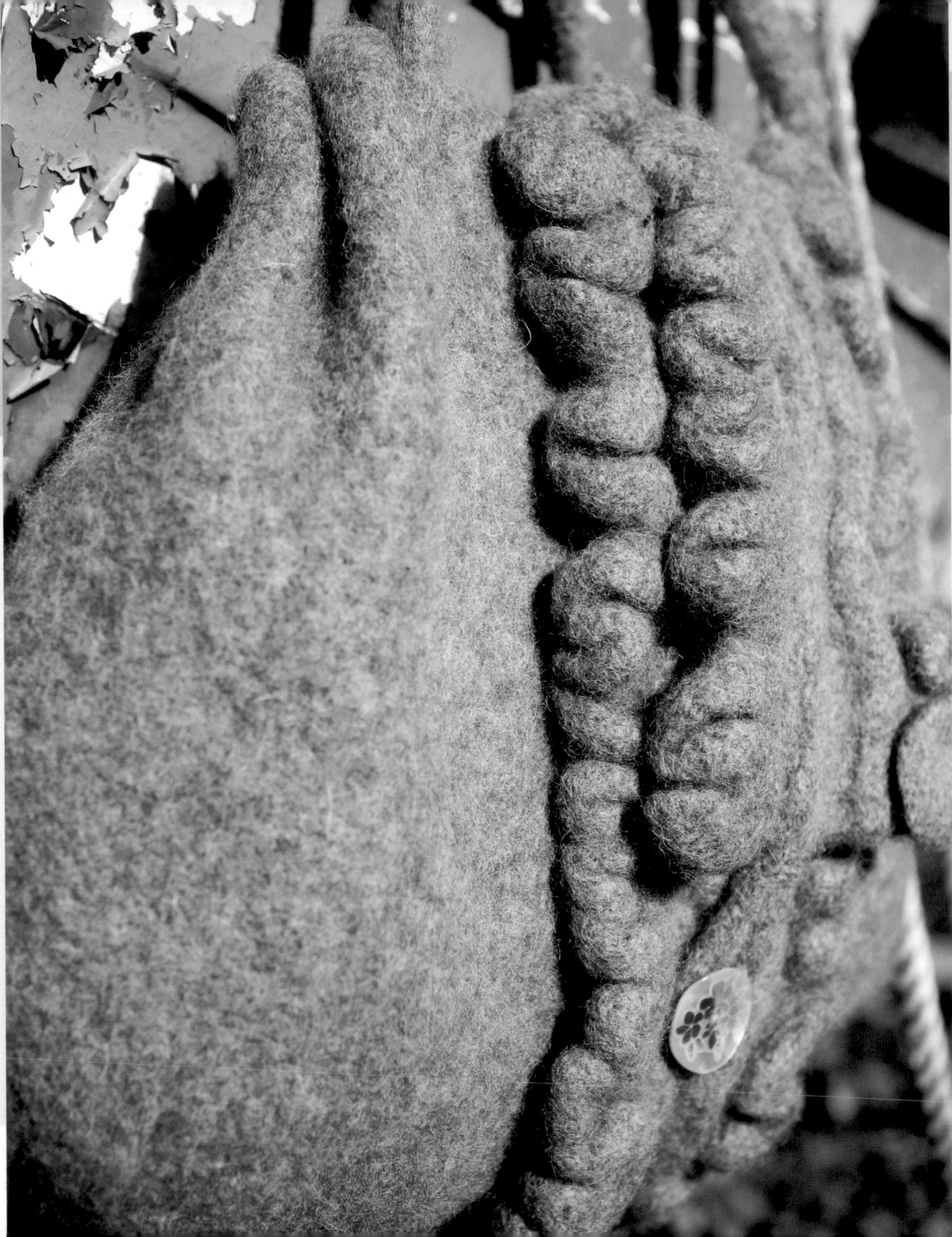

RIPPLE EFFECT

Spending an hour or two just watching the ripples on the sea is calming and offers an interlude of peace during the frenetic holiday season. It's also fun to drop a pebble into a pond and watch the ripples spreading out from where it fell. The ripples on the fastening band of this beautiful sea-blue bag are a reminder of happy summers.

COLOURS INCORPORATED

MATERIALS

❖ *500g aran-weight pure wool*

❖ *A pair of 5.5mm straight needles (US9:UK5)*

❖ *A 5.5mm circular needle (US9:UK5)*

❖ *A pair of 4.5mm double-pointed needles (US7:UK7)*

❖ *4 stitch markers*

❖ *Wool needle to finish off ends of yarn*

❖ *1 button (28–38cm)*

Note: our example was made using Sheepfold's Heather range aran in Wisteria, with an approx. 1in (28mm) diameter shell button.

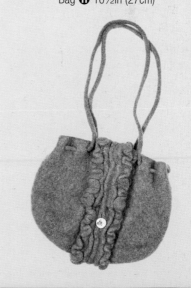

DIMENSIONS

BEFORE FELTING

Base **W** 16½in (42cm) Base **D** 6in (15.5cm)

Bag **H** 17in (43cm)

❖

AFTER FELTING

Base **W** 11¾in (30cm) Base **D** 4½in (11.5cm)

Bag **H** 10½in (27cm)

DIFFICULTY RATING ✪ ✪ ✪

SPECIAL TECHNIQUES

Garter stitch *see page 145*
Stocking stitch *see page 145*
Using stitch markers *see page 147*

Working in the round *see pages 148–9*
Making an I-cord *see page 150*
Felting *see page 152*

Frill *instructions below*

INSTRUCTIONS

This bag is worked in the round using a circular needle.

The base

Using the 5.5mm straight needles, cast on 58 sts and knit 40 rows in garter stitch. Change to the circular needle and knit across the sts from the straight needle. Pick up and knit 24 sts along the short edge of the base, 58 sts along the second long edge and 24 sts along the second short edge, placing a stitch marker at each corner (164 sts).

The sides

Knit 76 rounds, moving the markers across as they are reached, ending 1 st before the end of the round. At this point, the bag will be approximately 15in (38cm) high.

Eyelet round: Cast off 2 sts. *K6, cast off 2 sts**, repeat from * to ** once. K24, cast off 2 sts, repeat from * to ** seven times, k24, cast off 2 sts, repeat from * to ** four times, k6. Remove the markers, which will be in the centre of the corner cast-off sections. Place a safety pin to mark the start of the round.

Next round: Knit all stitches, casting on 2 sts over each cast-off section. There should now be eight eyelets at each end of the bag with one at each corner. Knit 6 more rounds.
Purl 1 round, knit 1 round, purl 1 round. Cast off all stitches k-wise.

> **TIP**
> When casting on with a large number of stitches, place a needle protector or a blob of adhesive putty on the opposite end of the circular needle to prevent any stitches falling off.

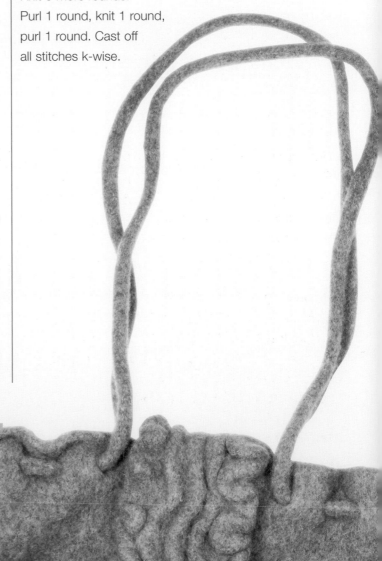

The handles

Using the 4.5mm double-pointed needles, cast on 6 sts and work in I-cord for 98in (250cm). Thread the handle through the eyelets, beginning from the outside at the start of a long central section (the 24 sts knitted in the eyelet round). When it has passed round the whole edge of the bag, sew the remaining 6 sts to the start of the I-cord to join into a single piece.

Fastening band

Using the 5.5mm circular needle, cast on 640 sts (you really *do* need that many). To keep count when casting on, it helps to place a marker on the needle every 100 sts. Remove the markers when working the first row.

Using the circular needle but working back and forth, k 1 row.
Next row: P2tog across the full length (320 sts).
Next row: K2tog across the full length (160 sts).
Starting with a purl row, work 28 rows in stocking stitch.
Next row: Increase in every stitch, p-wise (320 sts).
Next row: Increase in every stitch, k-wise (640 sts).
Purl 1 row, then cast off all stitches k-wise.

Trimming

Using the 4.5mm double-pointed needles, cast on 3 sts and work an I-cord 57in (145cm) long. Work a second, identical I-cord. Work a third I-cord 62in (157cm) long. Mark a point 4¾in (12cm) from the end of the longer I-cord and sew the end to it to form a loop.

Starting and ending the I-cords at the short edges of the fastening band, sew the three I-cords along the length of the fastening band in gentle ripples. Place the I-cord with the loop in the centre and overhanging one short edge of the band.

Note: do not sew the actual band to the bag yet, as the direction of the knitting is different and levels of shrinkage during felting may vary.

Finish off all ends of yarn on each piece by weaving into the work.

FELTING

Place the bag and the fastening band in separate bags or pillowcases to prevent them sticking together during felting. Felt in the washing machine. Our example felted sufficiently with two 140°F (60°C) washes.

Making up

Pin the end of the fastening band, without the loop, to the bag so it sits centrally at the top of one long side. Wind it carefully round the bag, pinning in place, until it reaches the top of the second long side. Leave the remaining length of the band free. Sew in place from the inside of the bag to minimize the appearance of the stitches on the outside.

Attach a button to the fastening band at a position aligned with the loop. If necessary, sew the loop together slightly for a snug fit.

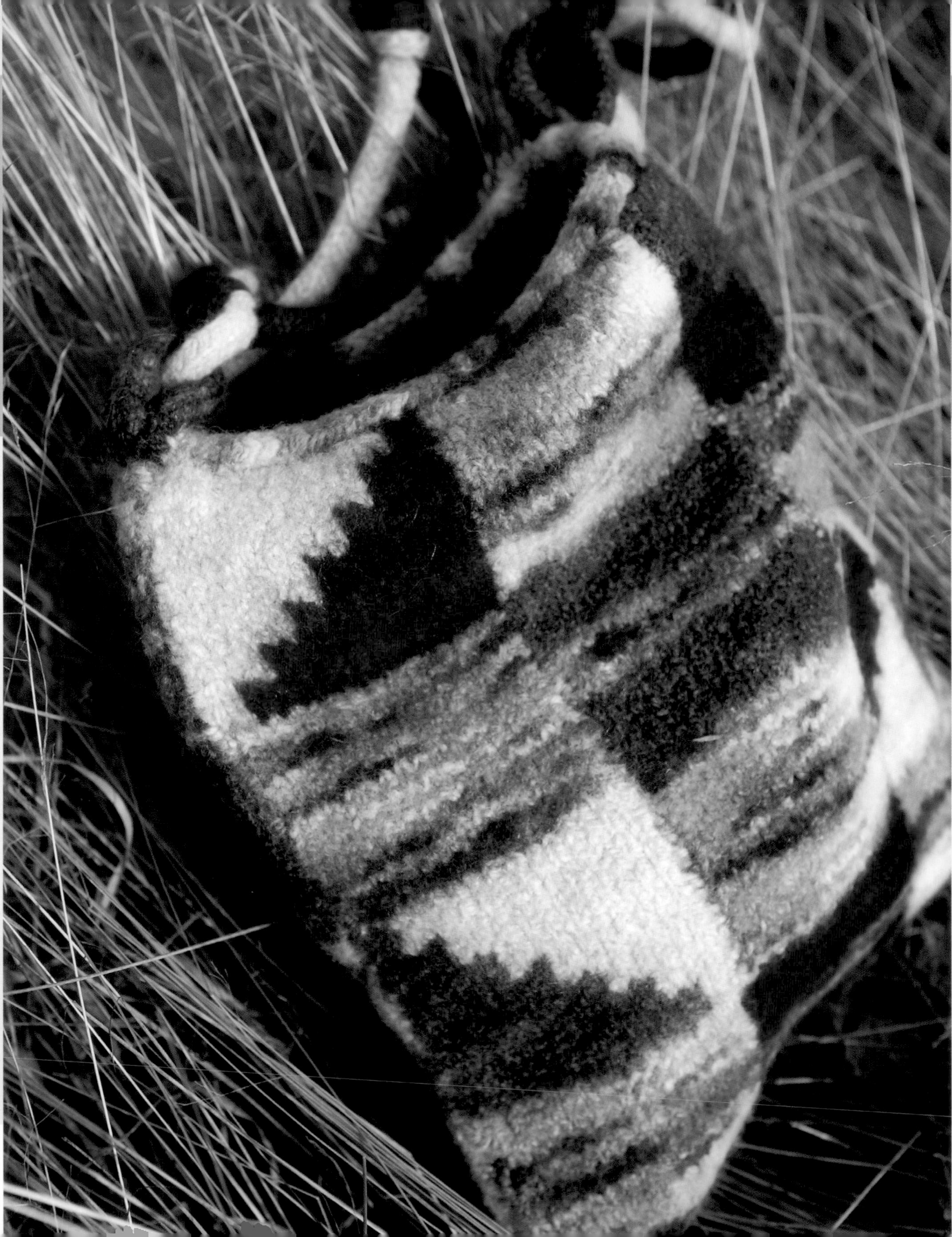

SAFARI

West African traditional fabrics are constructed by joining woven strips, each often only a few centimetres wide. The Ashanti, the major ethnic group in Ghana, are known for 'chequerboard' designs with geometric motifs, often in bright colours. This simple flat shoulder bag is made from long knitted strips that are sewn together.

COLOURS INCORPORATED

MATERIALS

❖ *100g aran-weight pure wool in main colour (M)*
   – variegated wool works well

❖ *50g aran-weight pure wool in each of three contrast colours*
   (C1, C2 and C3)

❖ *A pair of 5.5mm straight needles (US9:UK5)*

❖ *A pair of 4.5mm double-pointed needles (US7:UK7)*

❖ *Wool needle to sew bag pieces together and finish off ends of yarn*

Note: our main bag was made using Colinette Iona in Popsicle (M), with contrasts using Dali Shade in Purple Passion, Sunflower Susie and Vatican Pie. The variation was made using Jamieson's aran-weight Shetland wool in assorted natural shades.

DIMENSIONS

BEFORE FELTING
Ⓦ 12½in (31.5cm) Ⓗ 16½in (42cm)

❖

AFTER FELTING
Ⓦ 10in (25.5cm) Ⓗ 11½in (29cm)

DIFFICULTY RATING ✪ ✪

Chart for Safari

BLOCK A

BLOCK B

BLOCK C

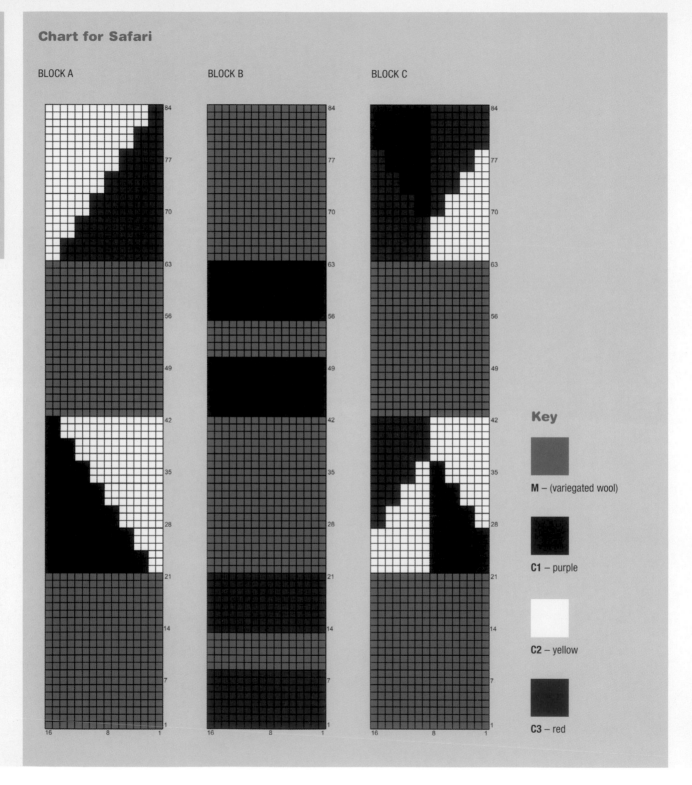

Key

M – (variegated wool)

C1 – purple

C2 – yellow

C3 – red

SPECIAL TECHNIQUES
Stocking stitch *see page 145*
Intarsia *see page 146*

Making an I-cord *see page 150*
Making an attached I-cord *see page 150*

Felting *see page 152*

INSTRUCTIONS

This bag is made from three long strips, knitted using the intarsia technique, then sewn together.

Body of bag

Using 5.5mm straight needles and M, cast on 16 sts. Work the 84 rows of pattern block A in stocking stitch using the intarsia technique, changing colour as indicated. Knit 2 rows in M. Repeat pattern block A. Cast off all stitches.

Using 5.5mm straight needles and C3, cast on 16 sts. Work the 84 rows of pattern block B in stocking stitch using the intarsia technique, changing colour as indicated. Knit 2 rows in M. Repeat pattern block B. Cast off all stitches.

Using the 5.5mm straight needles and M, cast on 16 sts. Work the 84 rows of pattern block C in stocking stitch using the intarsia technique, changing colour as indicated. Knit 2 rows M. Repeat pattern block C. Cast off all stitches.

Joining the strips

Slipstitch the three knitted strips together along the length, matching the garter strip line in M half-way along each strip. Don't worry if stitches are visible, as this is characteristic of woven, stripweave fabric. Fold the bag in half along the garter-stitch fold line and sew one of the side seams together.

Upper edge

Using the 4.5mm double-pointed needles and M, cast on 4 sts, then pick up and knit 1 st from the top of the bag, at the unsewn side, onto the same needle. Round the top of the bag, work in attached I-cord on these 5 sts, ending at the other side of the unsewn side seam. Cast off. Join the second side seam and the attached I-cord at the top.

With the outside of the bag facing, using C1 and the 4.5mm double-pointed needles, pick up and knit 5 sts from the junction of the attached I-cord and the cast-on/cast-off edge, at the top left-hand corner, as follows: 2 sts from the front, 1 st from the side seam and 2 sts from the back, so the 5 sts wrap around the side seam.

Work in I-cord on these stitches for 4¾in (12cm). Cast off. Sew the cast-off end to the start of the I-cord to form a secure loop. Repeat at the top right-hand corner of the bag.

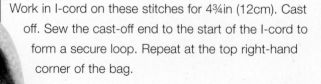

Handle

Using C2 and the 4.5mm double-pointed needles, cast on 4 sts and work in I-cord for 71in (180cm). Cast off. Using C3, make a second I-cord the same length.

Feed one of the I-cords through the loop at one side seam and knot to the second, leaving a tail approximately 2in (5cm) long. Knot the two cords together five times more along their length, approximately 9–10in (23–25cm) apart. Feed one of the cords through the second loop and knot the two ends together as before.

Note: the handle on this bag is designed to cross over the body. If you would prefer a shoulder bag reduce the length of the I-cords to 59in (150cm).

Making up

Finish off all ends of yarn by weaving into the work before felting.

FELTING

When knitted with Colinette's Iona, our example felted sufficiently with one 140°F (60°C) wash. When knitted with Jamieson and Smith's shetland wool, two 140°F (60°C) washes were needed.

INCA HAT

Simple geometric patterns have been found on ancient Inca artefacts and are now commonly used for hats with characteristic earflaps that are essential for keeping warm in the high Andes. The geometric designs, together with the shape of such hats, inspired this fun bag. You will need a lot of patience and an ability to keep count to complete this project, but the result is fabulous.

COLOURS INCORPORATED

MATERIALS

❖ 100g aran-weight pure wool in each of three colours (C1, C2 and C3)

❖ A 5.5mm circular needle (US9:UK5)

❖ A set of four 5.5mm double-pointed needles (US9:UK5)

❖ A pair of 5.5mm straight needles (US9:UK5)

❖ A pair of 4.5mm double-pointed needles (US7:UK7)

❖ Stitch marker

❖ Small amount of contrast yarn for markers

❖ Wool needle to finish off ends of yarn

❖ 10in (25cm) zip, plus matching sewing thread and needle (optional)

Note: our examples were made using Cascade 220 Wool. The main bag is in shades 9404 (C1), 2442 (C2) and 7822 (C3). The variation is in shades 8010 (C1), 8903 (C2) and 9467 (C3).

DIMENSIONS

BEFORE FELTING

Max **W** 14in (36cm)

H (excluding dangling I-cords) 20½in (52cm)

❖

AFTER FELTING

Max **W** 10½in (26.5cm)

H (excluding dangling I-cords) 14in (35.5cm)

DIFFICULTY RATING ⊕ ⊕ ⊕

SPECIAL TECHNIQUES

Garter stitch *see page 145*
Stocking stitch *see page 145*
Using stitch markers *see page 147*

Working in the round *see pages 148–9*
Making an I-cord *see page 150*
Felting *see page 152*

Attaching a zip *see page 154*

ABBREVIATIONS

m1: *make 1 stitch by picking up the loop lying between the last and next stitch and knitting into the back of it.*

mB: *knit, purl, knit, purl, knit and purl all in the first stitch. Turn work, k6 loosely. Turn, purl first 3 sts together, purl next 3 sts together, pass the first stitch over the second stitch and off the needle, leaving a single stitch and so completing the bobble.*

INSTRUCTIONS

Start by making three I-cords, then knit in the round using double-pointed needles. When there are enough stitches transfer to a circular needle if preferred.

The sides

Using two 5.5mm double-pointed needles and C1, cast on 5 sts and work in I-cord for 6in (15cm). Leave sts on the needle. Knit identical I-cords in C2 and C3 so there are I-cords in each of the three colours, each on a double-pointed needle.

The striped base

Round 1: Using C1, knit the 5 sts of each I-cord onto a single 5.5mm double-pointed needle (15 sts in total). Place a stitch marker on the needle to indicate the start of subsequent rounds. Divide sts across three double-pointed needles and work two rounds on them using C1.

Next round: Using C2, k1, (m1, k5) twice, m1, k4 (18 sts).

Knit one round without increases.

Next round: Using C3, k1, (m1, k3) five times, m1, k2 (24 sts).

Knit two rounds.

Next round: Using C1, k1, (m1, k4) five times, m1, k3 (30 sts).

Knit two rounds.

Next round: Using C2, k1, (m1, k5) five times, m1, k4 (36 sts).

Knit two rounds.

Next round: Using C3, k1, (m1, k4) eight times, m1, k3 (45 sts).

Knit three rounds.

Next round: Using C1, k1, (m1, k5) eight times, m1, k4 (54 sts).

Knit three rounds.

Next round: Using C2, k1, (m1, k6) eight times, m1, k5 (63 sts).

Knit three rounds.

Next round: Using C3, k1, (m1, k7) eight times, m1, k6 (72 sts).

Knit three rounds.

Next round: Using C1, k1, (m1, k6) eleven times, m1, k5 (84 sts).

Knit four rounds.

Next round: Using C2, k1, (m1, k7) eleven times, m1, k6 (96 sts).

Knit four rounds.

Next round: Using C3, k1, (m1, k8) eleven times, m1, k7 (108 sts). Knit four rounds.
Next round: Using C1, k1, (m1, k9) eleven times, m1, k8 (120 sts). Knit four rounds.
Next round: Using C2, k1, (m1, k10) eleven times, m1, k9 (132 sts). Knit four rounds.

If you wish to change to the circular needle you may wish to do so on the next round (if the double-pointed needles are short you may wish to do this sooner). Using C3 purl 4 rounds.
Using C1, make a fold by knitting each stitch in the round together with the loop at the back of the stitch lying 5 rounds below.
Knit 5 more rounds in C1.

The rest of the body

This is made using the six pattern blocks below. When using two colours in the same round, carry loose loops of contrast yarn across the back of your work. These pattern blocks can be knitted in any order and any colour combination, but ensure that the total number of rounds knitted is the same as the examples given (56 rounds).

NOTE
The examples are made using pattern 1 (C1 and C2), pattern 2 (C2 and C3), pattern 3 (C1 and C3), pattern 4 (C1 and C3), pattern 5 (C2 and C3), pattern 1 (C1 and C3), pattern 2 (C1 and C2), pattern 6 (C3 and C1), pattern 4 (C1 and C3) and finally pattern 5 (C1 and C2).

Pattern 1 (6 rounds)
Rounds 1 and 5: K1 in C1, *k2 in C2, k2 in C1**. Repeat * to ** to last three sts, k2 in C2, k1 in C1.
Rounds 2 and 6: *K2 in C1, k2 in C2**. Repeat * to ** to end of round.
Round 3: K1 in C2, *k2 in C1, k2 in C2**. Repeat * to ** to last three sts, k2 in C1, k1 in C2.
Round 4: *K2 in C2, k2 in C1**. Repeat * to ** to end of round.

Pattern 2 (6 rounds)
Rounds 1, 3 and 5: Knit all sts in C2.
Rounds 2, 4 and 6: Knit all sts in C3.

Pattern 3 (5 rounds)
Use short lengths of contrast yarn for the bobbles, breaking off yarn between each.
Rounds 1, 2, 4 and 5: Knit all sts in C1.
Round 3: K5 in C1, mB in C3, *k 11 in C1, mB in C3**. Repeat * to ** to last 6 sts. Knit to end in C1.

Pattern 4 (6 rounds)
Rounds 1, 3 and 5: *K1 in C1, k1 in C3**. Repeat * to ** to end of round.
Rounds 2, 4 and 6: *K1 in C3, k1 in C1**. Repeat * to ** to end of round.

Pattern 5 (5 rounds)
Rounds 1 and 5: *K2 in C2, k2 in C3**. Repeat * to ** to end of round.
Rounds 2 and 4: K1 in C3, *k2 in C2, k2 in C3**. Repeat * to ** to last three sts. K2 in C2, k1 in C3.
Round 3: * K2 in C3, k2 in C2**. Repeat * to ** to end of round.

Pattern 6 (5 rounds)
Rounds 1, 2, 4 and 5: Knit all sts in C3.
Round 3: *K5 in C3, mB in C1**. Repeat * to ** to end of round.

When you have worked the ten blocks of pattern (56 rounds), work a 4-round garter-stitch band (knit one round, purl one round, repeat once more) using C2 and ending at stitch marker.

Next round (eyelet): Still using C2, k4, cast off 5 sts, k47 (48 sts on needle since eyelet). Cast off 5 sts, k7 (8 sts on needle since last eyelet). Cast off 5 sts, knit to 9 sts before the end of the round. Cast off 5 sts, knit to end.
Next round: Knit to end casting on 5 sts over the sts previously cast off. You should now have 4 eyelets, two at each side of the bag.

Using C3, work a 6-round garter-stitch band (knit one round, purl one round, twice more. Cast off all stitches k-wise, marking the edge with contrast thread at the start of the round and at the midpoint between the eyelets on the opposite side of the bag, to assist in attaching the optional lid.

Lid (optional)
This is made in 2 sections and attached to the bag before felting. A zip is attached between the sections after felting.

Using the 5.5mm straight needles and the same colour as the first garter stitch band (C2 in our examples), cast on 63 sts. Knit 2 rows.
Next row: K2tog, knit to last 2 sts, k2tog.
Repeat this decrease row a further 5 times (51 sts).
Cast off all stitches.
Make an identical second piece.

Handle
Using C1 and the 4.5mm double-pointed needles, cast on 6 sts. Work in I-cord for 59in (150cm), alternating between C1, C2 and C3 on every row.
There is no need to break off the yarn between colours, simply keep the 3 colours passing up the back of the cord as you work. Remember to pull each colour firmly, but not tightly, before knitting a row with it. You will end up with the stripes in a diagonal spiral, a bit like a barbers pole! Cast off all sts.

Finishing off

Lay the bag flat with the two markers at either side edge. Pin one lid section to the inside of your bag, with the cast-off edge and the shaped sides attached to the bag and the cast-on edge unattached. This should be pinned to the garter-stitch ridge lying just below the eyelet row, with the ends of the shaped edges lying below the contrast markers placed when casting off at the top of the bag. Sew in place. Repeat for the second lid section on the other side of the bag, so creating a slit in which the zip will be sewn after felting. Remove the marker threads.

Lay the bag flat, matching the pairs of eyelets at each side. Mark a point 8in (20cm) from each end of the I-cord handle. Pass the I-cord through one pair of eyelet holes and firmly sew the end to the adjacent marker. Repeat with the other end of the I-cord and opposite pair of eyelet holes, so forming a loose loop at each end of the handle, attached to the bag through the eyelet holes.

Finish off all ends of yarn by weaving into the work before felting. If necessary, close up any hole at the base of the bag.

FELTING

Felt the bag in the washing machine. Our examples felted sufficiently with one 140°F (60°C) wash.

Attaching a zip

If you wish, sew a zipper into your bag, along the central edges of the lid, to give increased security during use.

VARIATION
Colours incorporated

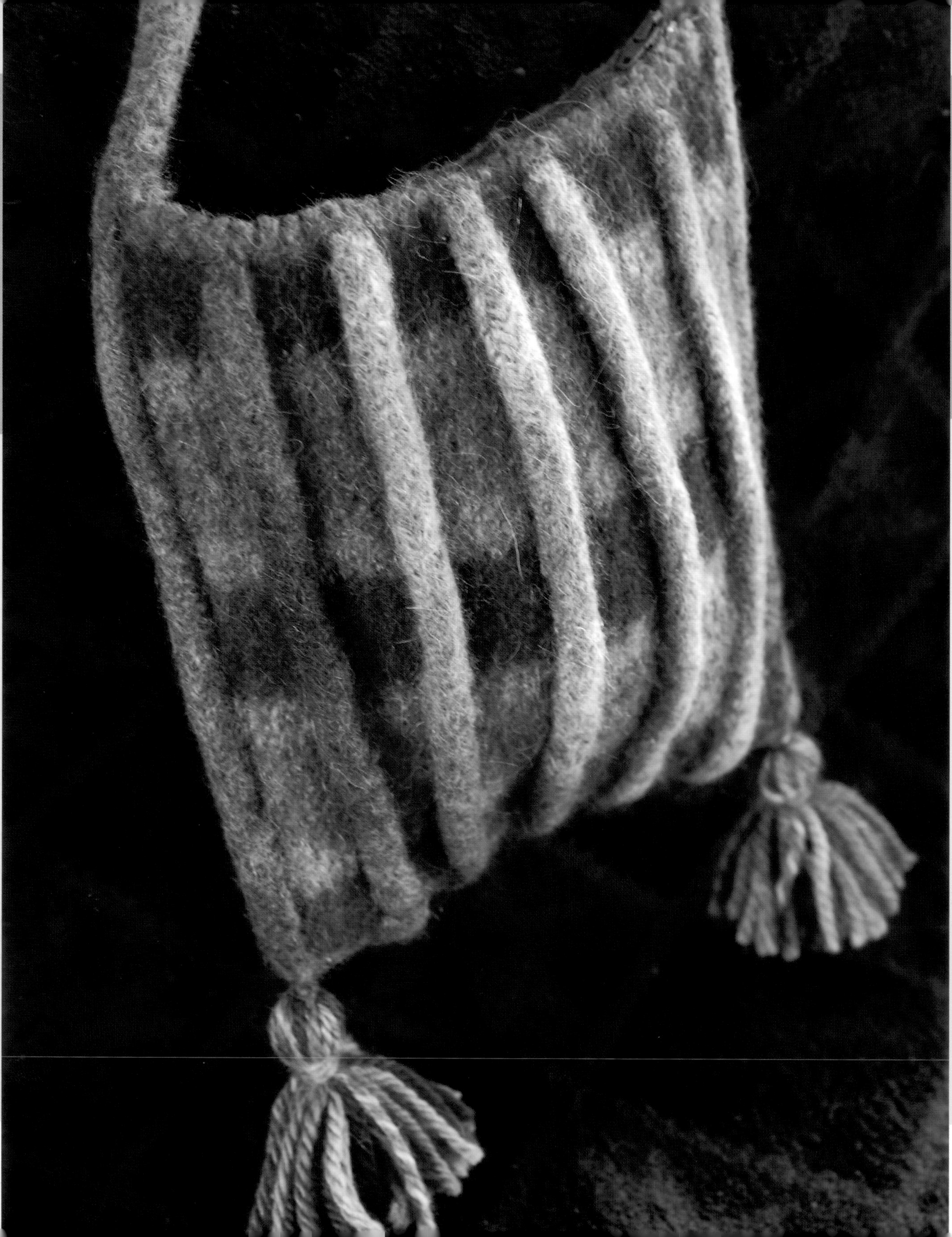

MEDINA

Moroccan architecture reflects elements of both Islamic and Spanish design. Geometric patterns, often in bright colours, are a common feature, though the natural red sandstone colours are also evident. Much decoration is calligraphic, which is, in itself, closely linked to geometry. The design of this bag uses the tones of red sandstone and mimics the pillars and ceilings of Moroccan buildings.

COLOURS INCORPORATED

MATERIALS

❖ *100g aran-weight pure wool in main colour (M) – variegated yarn is especially good*

❖ *50g aran-weight pure wool in three contrast colours (C1, C2 and C3)*

❖ *A pair of 5.5mm straight needles (US9:UK5)*

❖ *A pair of 4.5mm double-pointed needles (US7:UK7)*

❖ *Wool needle to finish off ends of yarn*

❖ *7in (18cm) zip and matching sewing thread (optional)*

Note: our example was made using Patons Jet wool/alpaca blend in orange blue 004 (M), orange 605 (C1), russet 708 (C2) and beige 102 (C3).

DIMENSIONS

BEFORE FELTING
Ⓦ 10¼in (26cm) Ⓗ 12¼in (31cm)

❖

AFTER FELTING
Ⓦ 7½in (19cm) Ⓗ 8in (21cm)

DIFFICULTY RATING ⊕

SPECIAL TECHNIQUES

Garter stitch *see page 145*
Stocking stitch *see page 145*

Making an I-cord *see page 150*
Felting *see page 152*

Attaching a zip *see page 154*
Making tassels *see page 156*

INSTRUCTIONS

Using the 5.5mm straight needles and C1 cast on 36 sts. Knit 2 rows in garter stitch. Change to C2 and knit a further 2 rows in garter stitch.

Work in stripe pattern in stocking stitch as follows:

6 rows C2
4 rows C3
10 rows C1
4 rows C3
10 rows C2
4 rows in C3
10 rows C1
4 rows C3
6 rows C2

Work 4 rows in garter stitch, using C1.

Work the second side of the bag in stocking stitch as follows:

6 rows C2
4 rows C3
10 rows C1
4 rows C3
10 rows C2
4 rows C3
10 rows C1
4 rows C3
6 rows C2

Top edge

Working in garter stitch, knit 2 rows in C2 and 2 rows in C1. Cast off all stitches.

Making up

You should now have a symmetrical patterned piece. Fold in half along the central garter-stitch section knitted in C1 so the stripes on the two sides match exactly. Join the side seams to complete the body of the bag.

The handle

Using M and the 4.5mm double-pointed needles, cast on 6 sts and work in I-cord for 71in (180cm). Cast off all stitches. Pin either end of the I-cord to the two side seams, aligning the cast-on/cast-off ends with the base of the bag. Sew the handle firmly to the two sides of the bag, along the full length of the side seams.

Decoration

Using M and the 4.5mm double-pointed needles, cast on 4 sts and work in I-cord until long enough to wrap round the bag from the top of one side to the top of the other. The top edges of the I-cord should sit at the boundary between the garter-stitch sections in C1 and C2.

Work four more I-cords of identical length. Spacing evenly, sew the I-cords in place to create a textured vertical stripe pattern on the bag, using vertical lines of stitches to help to keep them in straight lines.

Finish off all ends of yarn by weaving into the work before felting.

FELTING

Felt the bag in the washing machine. Our example felted sufficiently with one 140°F (60°C) wash.

Sewing in a zip (optional)

Sew a zip along the top edge of the bag if required for increased security.

Making tassels (optional)

Make and attach tassels to the bottom ends of the I-cord handle if desired. In our example, all four shades of yarn were used for the tassel and M used to secure the bundle and create its head.

Note: tassels must be attached after the bag is felted.

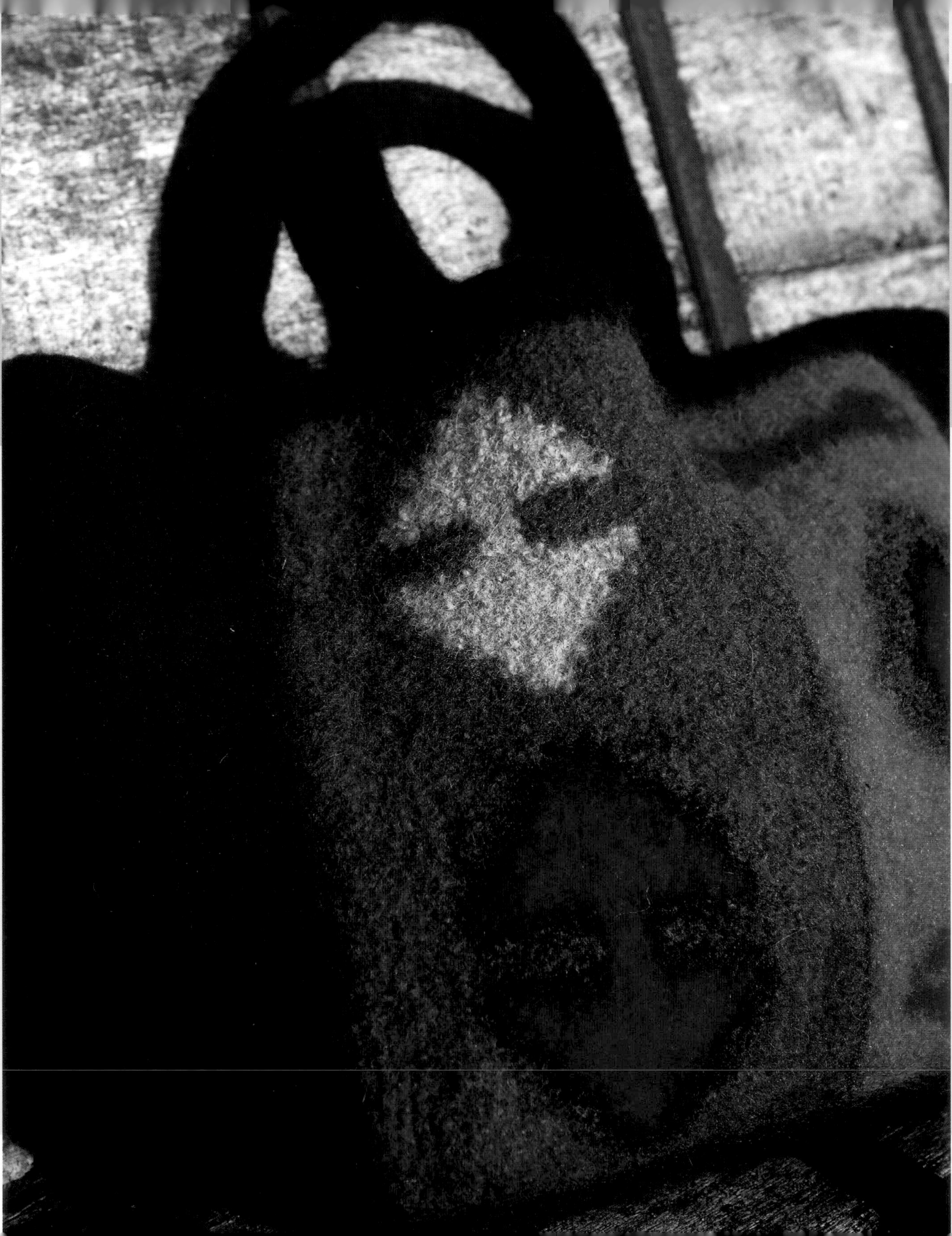

KILIM SHOPPER

The souks of Marrakesh are a stunning visual experience, with fabulous carpets hanging overhead in vibrant shades of red, orange, rust, blue and black. These kilim rugs tell stories, with each motif expressing a different meaning. The motifs that appear on this bag are variations of love, fertility, happiness, protection and immortality – so feel good as you make and use it!

COLOURS INCORPORATED

MATERIALS

❖ *300g chunky-weight pure wool in dark colour (M)*

❖ *100g chunky-weight pure wool in each of four contrast colours (C1, C2, C3 and C4)*

❖ *A pair of 8mm straight needles (US11:UK0)*

❖ *4 stitch holders*

❖ *Wool needle to sew seams and finish off ends of yarn*

Note: our example was made using Texere chunky wool in Black (M), plus Mustard, Red, Orange and Royal as contrasts.

DIMENSIONS

BEFORE FELTING
W 16¼in (41cm) Base **D** 8in (20.5cm)
Bag **H** 18¾in (47.5cm)

❖

AFTER FELTING
W 12¼in (31cm) Base **D** 6¾in (17cm)
Bag **H** 11½in (29cm)

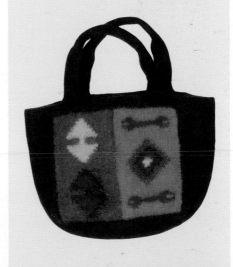

DIFFICULTY RATING ✪ ✪

Chart for Kilim Shopper

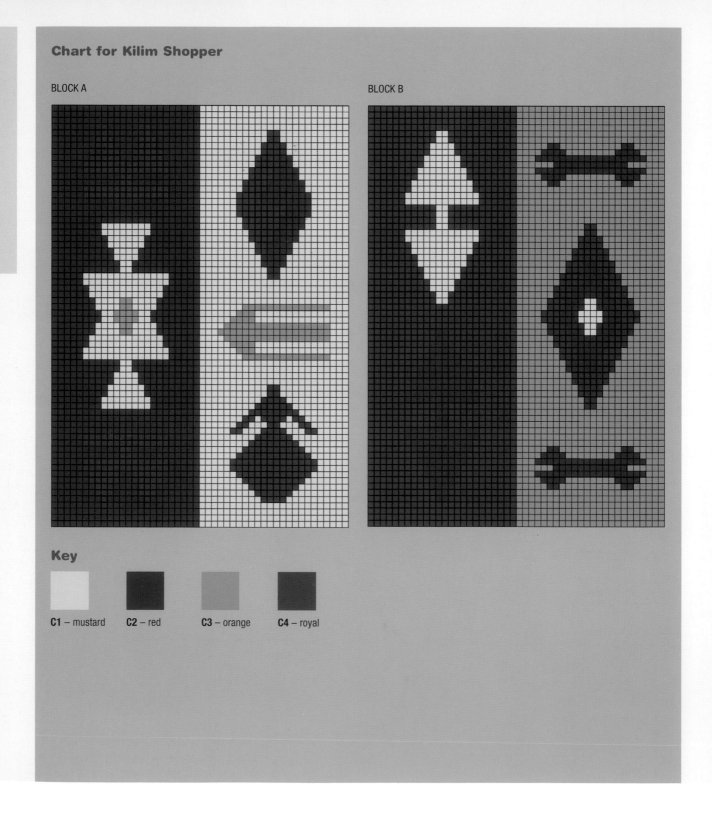

BLOCK A

BLOCK B

Key

C1 – mustard **C2** – red **C3** – orange **C4** – royal

SPECIAL TECHNIQUES

Garter stitch *see page 145*
Stocking stitch *see page 145*

Intarsia *see page 146*
Grafting stitches *see page 151*

Felting *see page 152*

INSTRUCTIONS

Before starting, wind a few small balls in each of the four contrast shades. When joining in each of these, leave 6–8in (15–20cm) of spare yarn at the beginning and end of each colour block to sew in later. Work the design in intarsia, not in fair-isle. If carrying the yarn across the back for 3 or 4 stitches, make sure you leave a good loop, i.e. do not pull across too tightly to allow for shrinkage of the yarn carried across the back.

The base

Using the 8mm straight needles and M cast on 48 sts and knit 40 rows in garter stitch.

The first side

Beginning with a knit row and joining in colours as necessary, work pattern block A in stocking stitch, starting from the bottom of the chart. Join in additional small balls of wool either side of each motif to avoid carrying lengths across the back of the design. Work until the 68-row design is complete.

Change to M and knit 8 rows to form a garter stitch top edge.

Next row: Cast off 4 sts, *K7 and place the 8 sts from the needle on a stitch holder**. Cast off 24 sts. Work * to ** once. Cast off the remaining 4 sts.

Note: there should now be two sets of 8 sts to form the handles.

The second side

With right side facing, pick up and knit 48 sts from the second long side of the base, working the first 24 sts in C3 and the remaining 24 sts in C4. Beginning with row 2, work pattern block B in stocking stitch. Work until the 68-row design is complete. Change to M and complete the top band and upper edge as before, again leaving two sets of 8 sts on stitch holders.

Side panels

With right side facing and using M, pick up and knit 28 sts from one of the short sides of the base. Starting with a purl row, work 67 rows in stocking stitch, then knit the 8-row garter-stitch top band. Cast off all stitches. Repeat for the second short side of the base.

The handles

Transfer the first set of 8 sts back to one of the 8mm straight needles. Rejoin M and work in garter stitch for 22¾in (58cm). Graft these stitches to the remaining 8 sts on the same long side of the bag, taking care not to twist the handle. Repeat for the handle on the other side.

Making up

Turn the bag inside out and join the four side seams, matching the garter-stitch and stocking-stitch sections. Sew in all loose ends of yarn. Sew up any large holes between colours but do not worry about keeping everything too neat and even. Fold one handle in half, lengthwise, and slipstitch the two edges together in the central portion (approx. one-third of the total length). This makes the wide handles easier to hold in the middle. Repeat for the second handle.

Finish off all ends of yarn on each piece by weaving into the work before felting.

FELTING

Felt the bag in the washing machine. Our example felted sufficiently with two 140°F (60°C) washes.

REVERSE SIDE
Colours incorporated

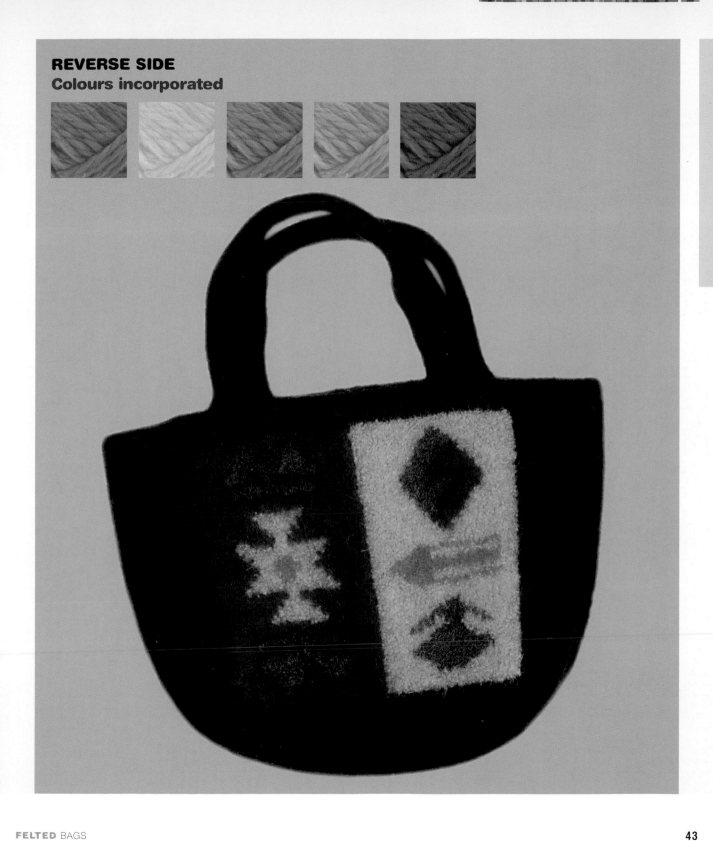

MOSAIC

Colourful Roman mosaic is found all across the Mediterranean region. The pieces fit together exactly with no overlaps or gaps and the effect is quite remarkable. This simple bag adapts the matching of shapes by adding a buttoned pocket that aligns with the buttoned flap.

COLOURS INCORPORATED

MATERIALS

- ❖ 200g DK-weight pure wool
- ❖ A pair of 4.5mm straight needles (US7:UK7)
- ❖ A pair of 4.5mm double-pointed needles (US7:UK7)
- ❖ Contrast yarn to mark rows
- ❖ 2 safety pins to indicate right side of work
- ❖ Wool needle to join pieces and finish off ends of yarn
- ❖ 2 buttons 1in (25mm) in diameter

Note: our examples were made using Twilley's Freedom Spirit in Bliss 508 (main bag) and Destiny 515 (variation).

DIMENSIONS

BEFORE FELTING
W 11½in (29cm) H 13¾in (35cm)

❖

AFTER FELTING
W 8in (20cm) H 8¼in (21cm)

DIFFICULTY RATING ⊕

SPECIAL TECHNIQUES
Garter stitch *see page 145*
Making an I-cord *see page 150*
Felting *see page 152*
Making tassels *see page 156*

INSTRUCTIONS

This simple bag is knitted in garter stitch throughout, with an I-cord handle.

The sides

Using the 4.5mm straight needles, cast on 50 sts and work 120 rows in garter stitch. The work should measure approx. 13in (34cm). Mark each end of the last row with contrast yarn to indicate the fold line. Work a further 120 rows in garter stitch, marking the ends of the last row to indicate the fold line at the top of the bag. *Note: to identify the right side of the work later, which can be difficult when working in garter stitch, attach a safety pin at an early stage.*

Work a further 40 rows in garter stitch.

Decrease pattern 1

Next row: *With right side facing, knit to last 2 sts, k2tog. Turn, k2tog, knit to end of row**.
Repeat * to ** eight more times (32 sts). This will shape along the left-hand edge, when the right side is facing.

The buttonhole

Next row: K8, cast off 6 sts, knit to last 2 sts, k2tog. Turn.
Next row: K2tog, knit to end of row, casting on 6 sts over the cast-off sts to complete the buttonhole (30 sts).

Note: now change to decrease pattern 2, which alters the shaping of the flap by bringing in decreases along the second side.

Decrease pattern 2

Next row: *With right side facing, k2tog, knit to last 2 sts, k2tog. Turn, k2tog, knit to end of row**.

Continue shaping using decrease pattern 2 until 3 sts remain. Sl1, K2tog, psso. Fasten off remaining stitch.

The pocket

Using the 4.5mm straight needles, cast on 40 sts and work 30 rows in garter stitch, again marking the right side of the work with a safety pin. Work decrease pattern 1 until 32 sts remain, then work a buttonhole as before (30 sts on needle). Mark the ends of the last row to help when attaching the pocket to the bag. Continue shaping using decrease pattern 2 until 3 sts remain. Sl1, K2tog, psso. Fasten off remaining stitch.

Making up

Fold the knitted piece at the first pair of markers with the top edge of the bag (cast-on edge) aligned with the second pair of markers. Sew the two side seams.

Sew the pocket to the bag, matching its lower right corner to the corner of the bag, so the oblique long edges of the bag and pocket run parallel. Sew the right-hand side seam as far as the marker and the lower edge of the pocket to the lower edge of the bag. Sew the shorter side edge to the front of the bag and continue along the oblique long sloping edge as far as the marker.

The handle

Using the 4.5mm double-pointed needles, cast on 6 sts and work in I-cord for 78½in (200cm). Cast off all stitches. Pin either end of the I-cord to the two side seams, with the cast-on/cast-off ends aligned with the base of the bag. Sew the handle firmly to the sides of the bag, taking care not to twist the cord, along the full length of the side seams.

Remove all markers and finish off ends of yarn by weaving into the work before felting.

FELTING

Felt the bag in the washing machine. Our examples felted sufficiently with one 140°F (60°C) wash.

Once dry, sew the buttons to the bag, aligning with the two buttonholes.

Tassels

If you wish, make and attach tassels to the bottom ends of the I-cord handle. These must be attached *after* your bag has been felted!

VARIATION
Colours incorporated

SKERRY

A skerry is a small rocky island found round the coast of Scotland; the name derives from the Old Norse *sker*, a rock in the sea. Many different natural shades of rock interlock to produce a wonderful mosaic rising from the waves. This design uses three shades of wool from the North Ronaldsay sheep, seen overleaf, that live on little more than a rocky outcrop.

COLOURS INCORPORATED

MATERIALS

❖ *100g aran-weight pure wool in main colour (M)*

❖ *50g aran-weight pure wool in contrast 1 (C1)*

❖ *50g aran-weight pure wool in contrast 2 (C2)*

❖ *A pair of 5.5mm needles (US9:UK5)*

❖ *A 5.5mm circular needle (US9:UK5)*

❖ *A pair of 4.5mm double-pointed needles (US7:UK7)*

❖ *4 stitch markers*

❖ *3 stitch holders or safety pins*

❖ *Wool needle to finish off ends of yarn*

Note: the version shown is made using Sheepfold's North Ronaldsay aran wool in Dark Brown (M), Grey and Sand.

DIMENSIONS

BEFORE FELTING

Base **W** 9in (23cm)   Base **D** 4in (10.5cm)

Bag **H** 11½in (29cm)

❖

AFTER FELTING

Base **W** 7¼in (18.5cm)   Base **D** 3in (8cm)

Bag **H** 8in (20cm)

DIFFICULTY RATING ✥ ✥ ✥

Chart for Skerry

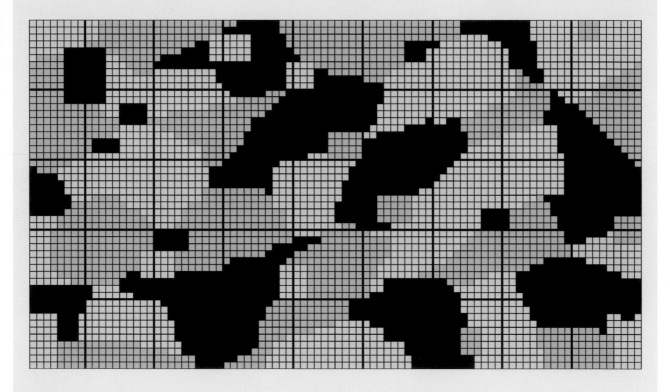

Key

M – dark brown   **C1** – grey   **C2** – sand

SPECIAL TECHNIQUES
Garter stitch *see page 145*
Stocking stitch *see page 145*
Intarsia *see page 146*

Using stitch markers *see page 147*
Working in the round *see pages 148–9*
Making an I-cord *see page 150*

Grafting stitches *see page 151*
Felting *see page 152*

INSTRUCTIONS

This design is worked back and forth on a circular
needle using the intarsia method. Before starting, wind
five smaller balls in each of the three colours. When
joining each of these in to form the pattern, leave 6–8in
(15–20cm) of spare yarn at the beginning and end of
each colour block to sew in later. When carrying the yarn
across 3 or 4 stitches, leave a full loop and do not pull
across too tightly. This is because during felting the wool
carried across will shrink in length more than the width
of your work.

The base

Using 5.5mm straight needles and M, cast on 32 sts
and work 24 rows in garter stitch. Change to the circular
needle and knit across the sts from the straight needle.
Pick up and knit 22 sts along the short edge of the
base, 32 sts along the second long edge and 22 sts
along the second short edge, placing a stitch marker
at each corner (88 sts).

Next round: Knit, moving the stitch markers across
as they are reached.

The sides

Using the chart and working from right to left, work the 88 sts of the first row of the pattern, temporarily removing the corner markers. Join in a small ball of wool each time a colour block is introduced. At the end of the row, turn and purl the second row of the pattern, working from left to right. Work the remaining 48 rows of the pattern in stocking stitch in the same way.

Next row: Using M, knit across all the stitches replacing the markers after 32 sts, then 12 sts, then 32 sts, then 12 sts (end).

The top edge

Rejoin the circle and work in the round. Knit 1 round, purl 1 round, knit 1 round, purl 1 round, ending at the stitch marker at the start of the round.

The handles

K7. Cast off 18 sts. *K4 and place the 5 sts from the needle on a stitch holder or safety pin**. Cast off 16 sts. Work * to ** once. Cast off 18 sts. Work * to ** once. Cast off 16 sts. Knit to end.

Note: there should now be four sets of 5 sts to form the handles, one set still on the circular needle. Each of these will be 2 sts after or before a corner stitch marker, on the long side of the bag.

Transfer the remaining 5 sts to a double-pointed needle and, using M, work in I-cord on these for 15in (38cm). Graft these stitches to the remaining 5 sts on the same long side of the bag.

Rejoin M and repeat for the handle on the other side.

Making up

Turn the bag inside out and join the open part of
the side seam of the pattern using slipstitch and
matching the colour block pattern. Sew in all loose
ends of yarn. Sew up any large holes between
colours but do not worry about keeping
everything too neat and even. Finish off all
ends of yarn on each piece by weaving into
the work before felting.

FELTING

Felt the bag in the washing machine.
Our example felted sufficiently with
two 140°F (60°C) washes.

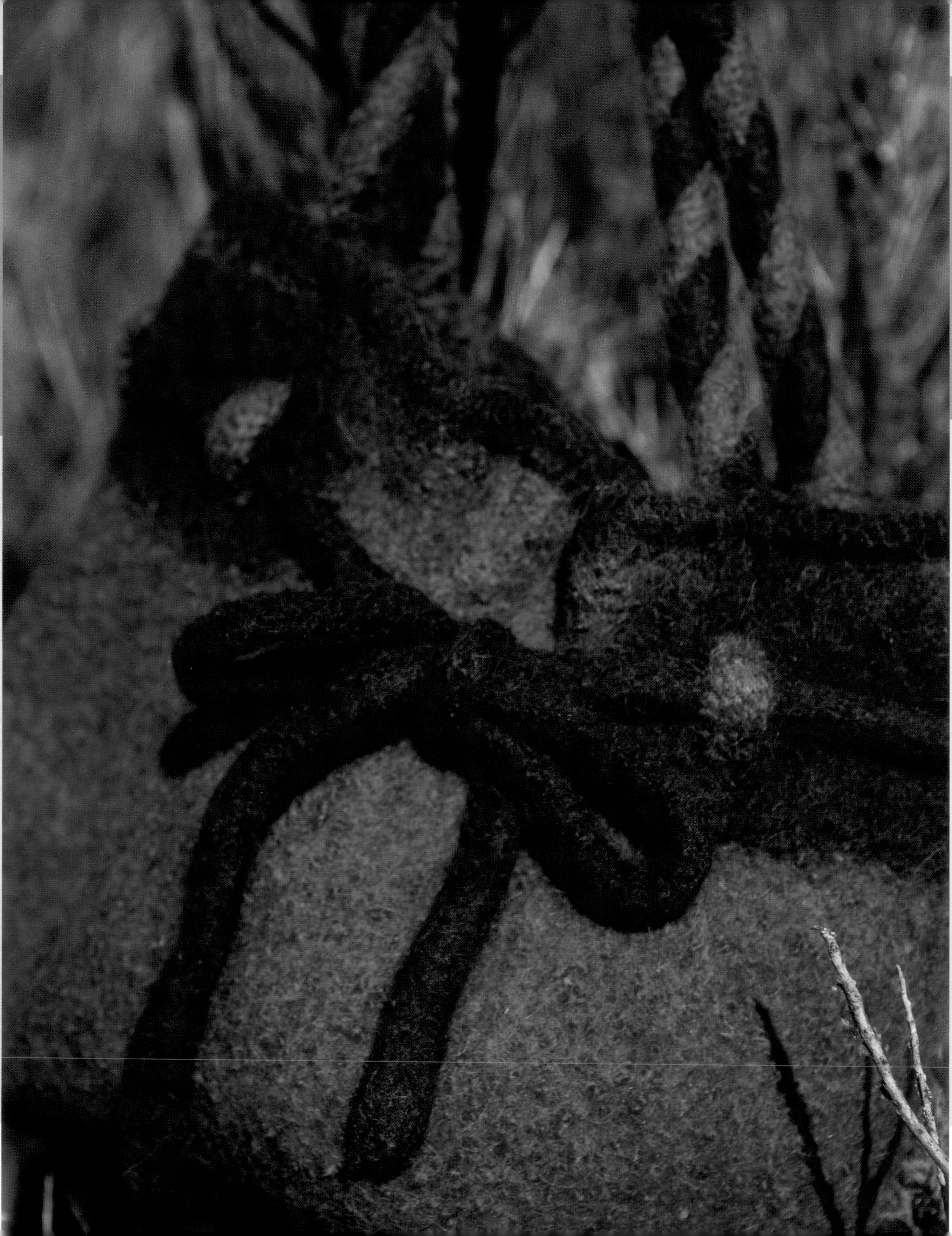

PERUVIAN

Fabulous alpaca and llama fibres from South America, particularly Peru, are increasingly available. It is said that knitting spread to Peru in the sixteenth century with the Conquistadores, but there are earlier references to single-needle knitting in fringing. This bag was inspired by the beautifully soft, camelid fibres, and reflects the colourful woven belted skirts traditionally worn by Peruvian women.

MATERIALS

❖ 250g (main bag) or 300g (variation) aran-weight pure wool in main colour (M)

❖ 150g aran-weight pure wool in contrast colour (C)

❖ A pair of 5.5mm straight needles (US9:UK5)

❖ A 5.5mm circular needle (US9:UK5)

❖ A pair of 4.5mm straight needles (US7:UK7)

❖ A pair of 4.5mm double-pointed needles (US7:UK7)

❖ 4 stitch markers

❖ Wool needle to attach bands and finish off ends of yarn

Note: our main bag was made using Mirasol Miski in Copper (M) and Wine (C). The variation was made using Wensleydale Longwool in Moonlight (M) and Denim (C).

DIMENSIONS

BEFORE FELTING
Base **W** 15½in (39cm) Base **D** 4¾in (12cm)
Bag **H** 15½in (39cm)

❖

AFTER FELTING
Base **W** 9½in (24cm) Base **D** 3½in (9cm)
Bag **H** 9½in (24.5cm)

DIFFICULTY RATING ⊕ ⊕ ⊕

Chart for Peruvian

Handle sewn to
inside of bag

long side of bag

short side
of bag

Key

Corner of bag – using marker at top to find this position

INSTRUCTIONS

This bag is worked in the round using a circular needle.

The base

Using 5.5mm straight needles and C, cast on 52 sts and knit 34 rows in garter stitch. Change to the circular needle and knit the sts from the straight needle. Pick up and knit 22 sts along the short edge of the base, 52 sts along the second long edge and 22 sts along the second short edge, placing a stitch marker at each corner (148 sts).

The sides

Change to M and knit 75 rounds, moving the markers across as they are reached. At this point the bag will be approximately 15in (38cm) high.
Change to C and knit 1 round, purl 1 round, knit 1 round.
Cast off all stitches but leave a marker at each of the four corners to aid the placement of handles later.

The side panels

Using the 5.5mm straight needles and C, cast on 40 sts.
Row 1: Knit, increasing 1 st at each end of work (42 sts).
Row 2: Purl, increasing 1 st at each end of work (44 sts).
Row 3: Knit all stitches.
Row 4: Purl, increasing 1 st at each end of your work (46 sts).
Work 10 rows in stocking stitch, without further increase.

Row 15: Knit, decreasing 1 st at each end of work (44 sts).
Row 16: Purl all stitches.
Row 17: Knit, decreasing 1 st at each end of work (42 sts).
Row 18: Purl, decreasing 1 st at each end of work (40 sts).
Cast off all stitches.
Work a second identical piece.

Tabs for tie

Using the 4.5mm straight needles and M, cast on 8 sts. Knit 2 rows, then cast off all sts. Work a further five tabs, to give a total of six.

The tie

Using the 4.5mm double-pointed needles and C, cast on 6 sts and work in I-cord for 69in (175cm). Cast off.

The handles

Using the 4.5mm double-pointed needles and M, cast on 5 sts and work in I-cord for these for 27½in (70cm). Cast off.

Work a second piece in M and two identical pieces in C, giving a total of four cords.

To assemble and attach the first handle, lay one I-cord in M and one I-cord in C over each other and join at the end. Place the joined cords so the bottom edge is 8 sts down from the top of the M portion of the bag, and 2 sts in from the corner marker, along the long side (see chart). Sew in place up to the contrast band at the top of the bag, using M so the stitches are not evident on the outside once felted. Twist the two cords together and sew to the bag at the opposite end of the long side as before.

Repeat with the remaining 2 cords to create a handle on the opposite long side of the bag.

Making up

Lay the bag flat, matching the pair of handles to give a symmetrical design. Fold each panel in half and mark the centres. Align the centre of one side panel with one side fold and wrap round the outside of the bag, with the top edge 4 sts down from the start of the contrast band. Pin in place. Repeat with the second panel. There should be a gap of approximately 8in (20cm) between the curved ends of the two bands. Sew the two side panels in place.

Sew the top and bottom of three tie tabs in place on each side panel – one where each handle attaches to the bag and one centrally between these two positions. These should sit centrally from top to bottom of the side panels.

Pleat the two central portions between the ends of the two bands to reduce the width by approximately half. Three or four pleats will be sufficient. Catch in place using M.

Finish off all ends of yarn by weaving into the work before felting.

FELTING

Felt the bag and tie in the washing machine, each in separate mesh bags or pillowcases. For the main bag, make sure that the maximum temperature used is 86°F (30°C), as the baby llama felts so readily. Our main bag felted sufficiently with one 86°F (30°C) wash. For the variation using Wensleydale Longwool, one 140°F (60°C) wash is required.

Finishing

After felting, insert the tie through the tabs and tie in a bow at the centre front. Leave the bag to dry in a warm place. The bow can be adjusted as required or when you want more room at the top edge.

Note: the main bag is a particularly 'friendly' bag, as a percentage of every sale of Mirasol yarn is invested in the establishment and running of a boarding house for local children in Peru. It also requires a single, very low temperature wash to felt!

VARIATION
Colours incorporated

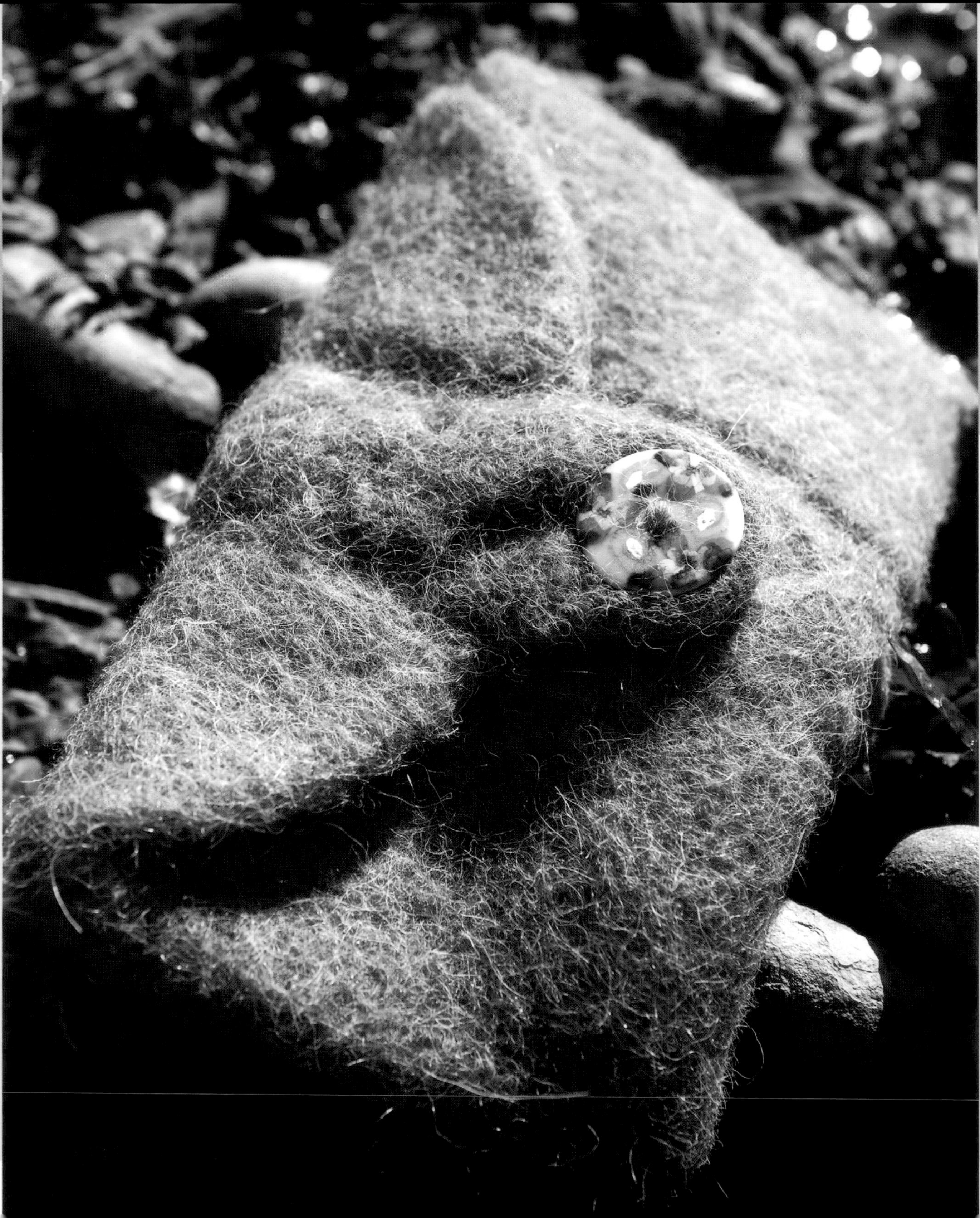

CABLE CLUTCH

Cable patterns are a traditional way to add texture to knitting, giving the appearance of twisted ropes. These patterns were handed down from mother to daughter for generations and, like the children's party game Chinese Whispers, would be adapted and changed. This bag is decorated with a simple two-rope pattern – but be careful not to felt it too much or the texture will disappear!

COLOURS INCORPORATED

MATERIALS

- ❖ 100–200g aran-weight pure wool
- ❖ A pair of 5.5mm straight needles (US9:UK5)
- ❖ A pair of 4.5mm double-pointed needles (US7:UK7)
- ❖ Stitch holder
- ❖ Contrast yarn to mark rows
- ❖ Wool needle to attach bands and finish off ends of yarn
- ❖ Large button, approx. 1½in (40mm) in diameter

Note: our main bag was made using 200g Cascade's Pastaza in Mauve Heather (075) and Incomparable Buttons' round button L473. The variation was made using 100g Mirasol Miski in Bluebell (105) and Incomparable Buttons' oval button L512.

DIMENSIONS

BEFORE FELTING
Ⓦ 10in (25.5cm) Ⓗ 7½in (19cm)

❖

AFTER FELTING
Ⓦ 8¾in (22.5cm) Ⓗ 5¼in (13.5cm)

DIFFICULTY RATING ⊕

SPECIAL TECHNIQUES
Garter stitch *see page 145*
Making an I-cord *see page 150*

Grafting stitches *see page 151*
Felting *see page 152*

Cable design *instructions below*

INSTRUCTIONS

This bag is worked on straight needles. The curved flap is a continuation of the body of the bag.

The sides

Using the 5.5mm straight needles cast on 49 sts and knit 2 rows in garter stitch. Work the following 20-row cable design a total of four times:

Cable design

Rows 1, 3, 5, 7, 9, 11, 15 and 17: K15, p3, k6, p1, k6, p3, k15.

Row 2 and all even numbered rows: P15, k3, p6, k1, p6, k3, p15.

Rows 13 and 19: K15, p3, slip 6 sts onto a double-pointed needle and hold at front of work, k6, p1, k6 from the double-pointed needle, p3, k15.

When the four blocks of pattern have been worked, place a marker at each end of the last row. At this point the work will measure approximately 15in (38cm).

The curved flap

Continue in cable design, decreasing one stitch at either edge on rows 5, 9, 12, 15, 17, 19, 20 and 21 as follows:

Decreasing on right side: K1, k2tog, pattern until 3 sts remain, k2tog, k1.

Decreasing on wrong side: P1, p2tog, pattern until 3 sts remain, p2tog, p1.

Next row: P1, p2tog, p2tog, pattern until 5 sts remain, p2tog, p2tog, p1.

Next row: K1, k2tog, k2tog, pattern until 5 sts remain, k2tog, k2tog, k1.

Next row: Cast off 4 sts, knit to end.

Next row: Cast off 6 sts, k5 (6 sts now on needle). Place these 6 sts on a stitch holder, k2tog, k5, cast off remaining stitches.

Break yarn and transfer the remaining 6 stitches to a 4.5mm double-pointed needle.

With right side facing, rejoin yarn and work in I-cord on these 6 stitches for 4in (10cm). Graft these stitches to the 6 stitches on the stitch holder to form a loop.

Making up

Fold the knitted piece so the garter-stitch band aligns with the two contrast markers and sew the two side seams formed. Remove the two contrast markers and finish off all ends by weaving into the work before felting.

FELTING

For yarn containing llama, use a low temperature to felt. Our main bag felted sufficiently with a single wash at 104°F (40°C). The variation needed only one wash at 86°F (30°C).

Attaching button

Sew the button to the bag, aligning with the I-cord loop.

VARIATION
Colours incorporated

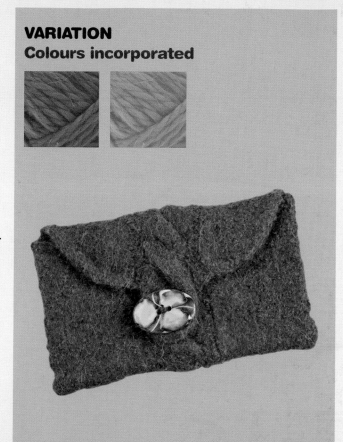

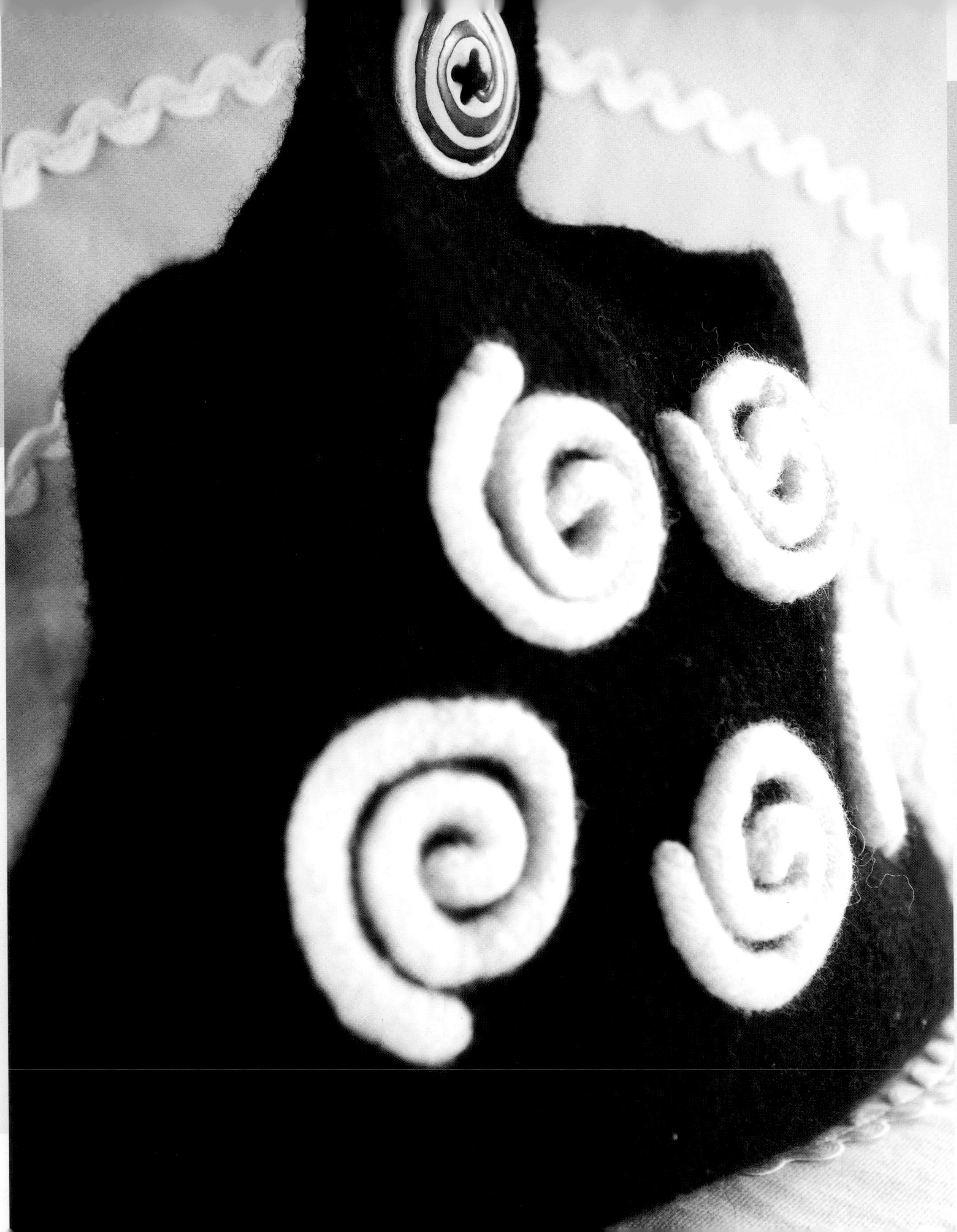

LIQUORICE ALLSORT

Why do so many childhood memories include food? And who can forget the joy of sharing a bag of liquorice allsorts or liquorice swirls, or the giggling caused by the temporary colouring of teeth afterwards? This bag reflects the black and white shades of liquorice allsorts and the shape of liquorice swirls. Yummy!

COLOURS INCORPORATED

MATERIALS

❖ *250g aran-weight pure wool in main colour (M)*

❖ *50g aran-weight pure wool in contrast colour (C)*

❖ *A pair of 5.5mm straight needles (US9:UK5)*

❖ *A pair of 4.5mm double-pointed needles (US7:UK7)*

❖ *4 stitch markers made from contrast yarn*

❖ *Stitch holder*

❖ *Wool needle to join side seams and finish off ends of yarn*

❖ *2 large buttons approx. 1¾in (45mm) in diameter*

❖ *Sewing needle and thread to attach spirals to bag*

Note: our example was made using Texere Airedale Aran in Black (M) and Cream (C) and Incomparable Buttons' round button L335.

DIMENSIONS

BEFORE FELTING
Base **W** 17¼in (44cm) Base **D** 4¾in (12cm)
Bag **H** 20½in (52cm)

❖

AFTER FELTING
Base **W** 11½in (29cm) Base **D** 4in (10cm)
Bag **H** 13½in (34cm)

DIFFICULTY RATING ⊕ ⊕

SPECIAL TECHNIQUES

Garter stitch *see page 145*

Stocking stitch *see page 145*

Using stitch markers *see page 147*

Making an I-cord *see page 150*

Grafting stitches *see page 151*

Felting *see page 152*

Cufflink-style fastening *instructions below*

ABBREVIATION

p2tog tbl: *purl 2 stitches together through back of loop*

INSTRUCTIONS

This bag is worked using straight needles. The spiral decoration is completed after felting.

The base

Using 5.5mm straight needles and M, cast on 65 sts and knit 34 rows in garter stitch.

Shape the front and back of the bag using the following 4-row pattern:

Row 1: Knit.

Row 2: Purl.

Row 3: Knit.

Row 4: P2tog, purl to last 2 stitches, p2tog tbl.

Repeat rows 1 to 4 until there are 31 sts on the needle. Place a marker at each end of the last row. Markers will remain in place to indicate where the upper edges of the sides are positioned. Continue rows 1 to 4 until there are 21 sts on the needle.

Next row: K6, cast off 9 sts, knit to end.

Next row: Purl to end, casting on 9 sts over the cast-off stitches to form buttonhole.

Work rows 3 and 4, then continue rows 1 to 4 until there are 9 sts on the needle. Place these sts on a holder.

With right side facing, pick up and knit 65 sts from the second long side of the base. Starting with row 2, complete the second side to match the first, again creating a 9-st buttonhole.

The handle

Work in garter stitch on the 9 sts left on the needle until the band measures 13in (33cm). For a longer handle knit until the band measures 29½in (75cm). Graft these 9 sts to those left on a holder from the first side.

The side panels

With right side facing, pick up and knit 21 sts from one of the short sides of the garter stitch base. Starting with a purl row, work 71 rows in stocking stitch. At this point, the side will measure approx. 13½in (34cm) from the base. Knit 4 rows. Cast off all stitches. Repeat on the second short side.

Making up

Sew the side panels to the front and back, matching the top edge of the two side panels with the contrast yarn markers on the edges of the front and back triangles.

Adding the spirals

Using the 4.5mm double-pointed needles and C, cast on 4 sts and work in I-cord for 12in (30cm). Cast off. Work a further four I-cords the same length, giving five in total.

Finish off all ends of yarn on each spiral and on the bag by weaving into the work before felting. Do not sew the spirals to your bag at this stage.

FELTING

Felt the bag in the washing machine. Our example felted sufficiently with a single 140°F (60°C) wash. Felt the contrast I-cords in a separate wash to avoid transfer of any colour from the bag. Wind the five I-cords into spirals. Leave to dry.

Finishing and fastening

When dry, sew the five spirals to the front of the bag as shown in the photograph.

Cufflink-style fastening

Join the two large buttons together with a length of M, leaving a gap of ½in (1–2cm) between buttons. Wind the wool round the central section between the buttons to make the attachment more secure. Pass each of the buttons through the two buttonholes to create a simple closure.

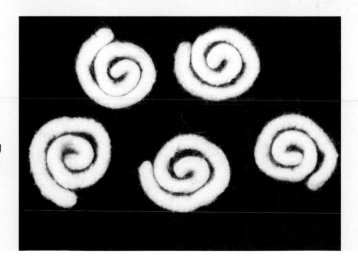

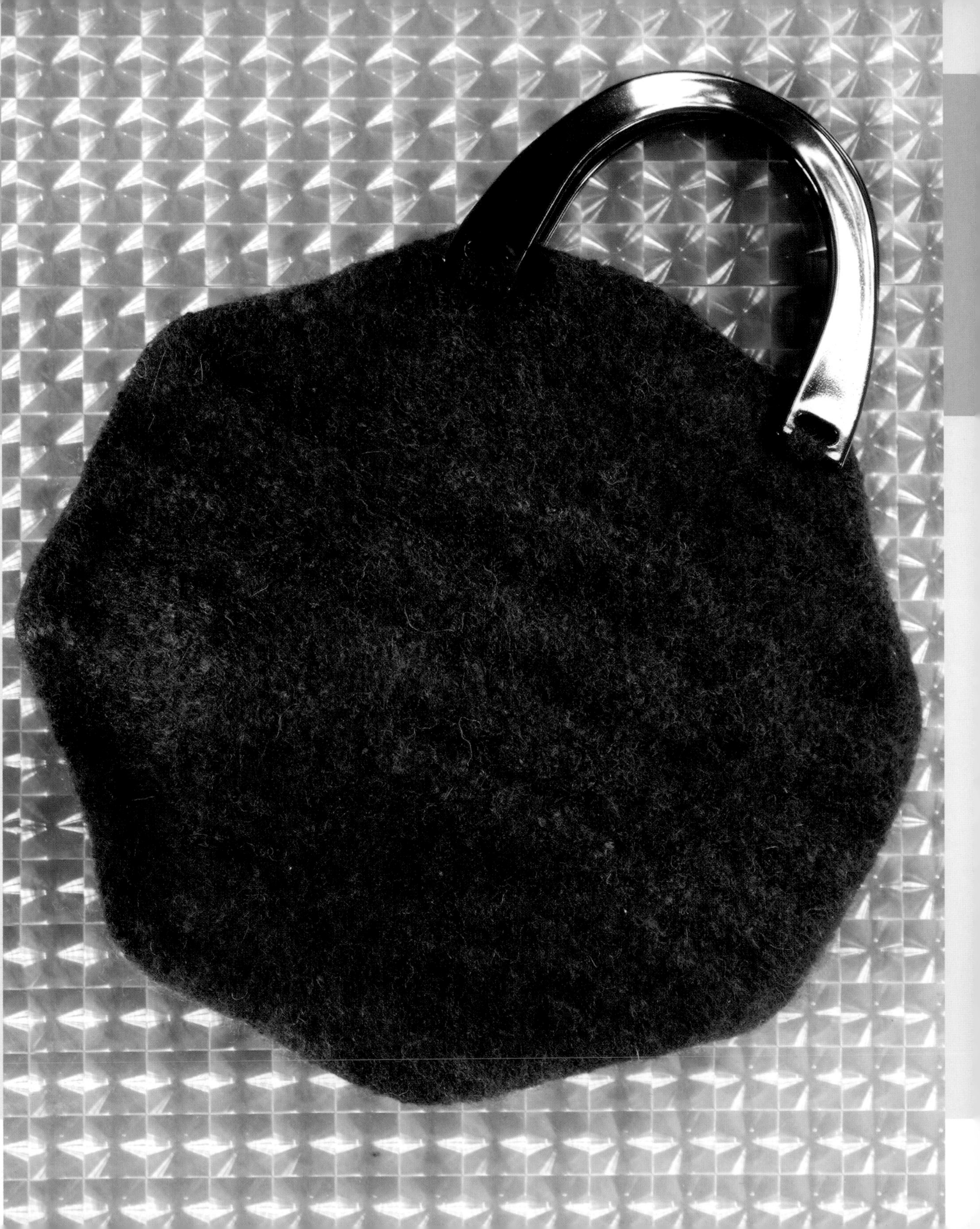

OCTAGON

We both have backgrounds underpinned by scientific training, so regular geometric shapes always appeal. Translating these into knitted, felted bags is sometimes a bit of a challenge, and this simple octagon is no exception. Don't worry if it does not look truly octagonal during the knitting stage: after felting its true shape will be revealed.

COLOURS INCORPORATED

MATERIALS

❖ *200g DK-weight pure wool*

❖ *A pair of 4.5mm straight needles (US7:UK7)*

❖ *A pair of 4.5mm double-pointed needles (US7:UK7)*

❖ *Wool needle to join work and finish off ends of yarn*

❖ *Pair of bag handles, maximum base width 6in (15cm)*

Note: our example was made using Twilley's Freedom Spirit in Desire (518) and Prym's 'Marilyn' handles.

DIMENSIONS

BEFORE FELTING

Max **W** 18in (45.5cm) Max **H** 21in (53cm)

❖

AFTER FELTING

Max **W** 11½in (29cm) Max **H** 11in (28cm)

DIFFICULTY RATING ⊕

ABBREVIATION

m1: *make 1 stitch by picking up the loop lying between the last and next stitch and knitting, or purling, into the back of it.*

INSTRUCTIONS

An attached I-cord is worked on seven sides of the finished bag to give a neat, defined edge.

The bag

Using the 4.5mm straight needles, cast on 36 sts. Work the 6-row increase pattern below to give 44 stitches on the needle.

Increase pattern

Row 1: Knit all stitches.

Row 2: P1, m1, purl to last stitch, m1, p1.

Row 3: K1, m1, knit to last stitch, m1, k1.

Row 4: Purl all stitches.

Row 5: K1, m1, knit to last stitch, m1, k1.

Row 6: P1, m1, purl to last stitch, m1, p1.

Repeat rows 1 to 6 six more times (92 sts).
Work 52 rows in stocking stitch for the central panel, then work the decrease pattern below to give 84 stitches on the needle.

Decrease pattern

Row 105: K1, k2tog, knit to last 3 stitches, k2tog, k1.

Row 106: P1, p2tog, purl to last 3 stitches, p2tog, p1.

Row 107: Knit all stitches.

Row 108: P1, p2tog, purl to last 3 stitches, p2tog, p1.

Row 109: K1, k2tog, knit to last 3 stitches, k2tog, k1.

Row 110: Purl all stitches.

Repeat rows 105 to 110 six times more (36 sts).
Cast off all stitches.
Work a second side to match.

The edging

Join the front and back pieces on seven of the eight sides, leaving the two matched cast-off edges open.

Using the 4.5mm double-pointed needles, cast on 4 sts. Pick up and knit, onto the same needle, 1 st from the top of the bag where the joined sides meet the open side. Work round the seven sewn sides of the bag in attached I-cord on these stitches, starting at one side of the opening and ending at the other. Take care to work along the sewn seam. Cast off all stitches. Finish off ends of yarn by weaving into the work before felting.

FELTING

Felt the bag in the washing machine. Our example felted sufficiently with two 140°F (60°C) washes. As this is a flat shape, it may be necessary to pull the front and back of the bag apart, firmly, between washes and at the end. Run a finger along the seven sewn sides, inside the bag, to separate the two pieces up to the attached I-cord edging.

Attaching the handles

When the bag is fully dry, sew on the handles with the base placed approximately 1in (2.5cm) below the top edge of the bag. Take care to align the handles on the front and back of the bag for a tidy result. Matching yarn was used for the example, but contrast yarn may be used if preferred.

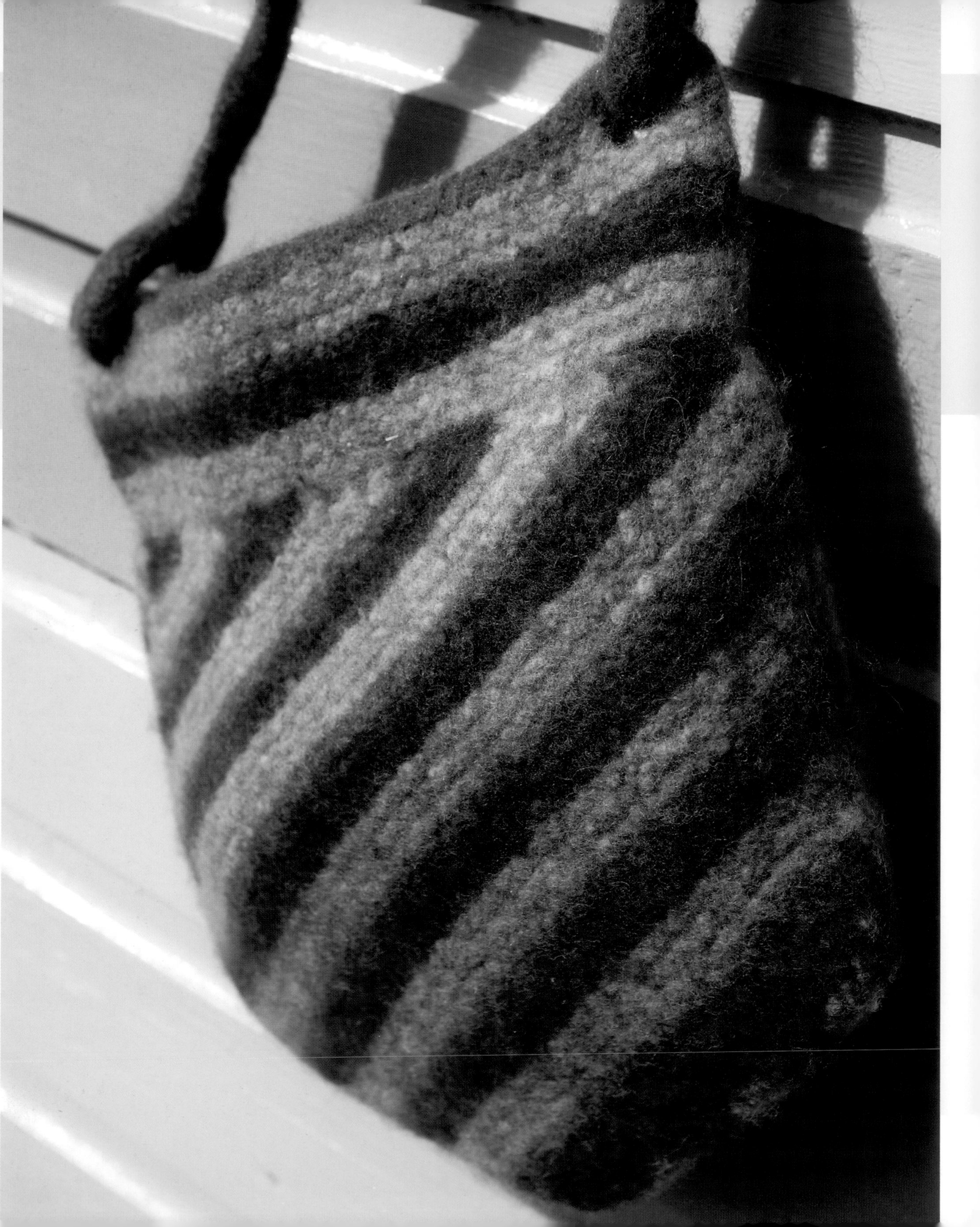

NECKTIE

The fashion for ties has a long history. Wide ties became popular in the 1960s and '70s and young men often wrapped the knot many times to produce a 'fat tie'. An inevitable side-effect of this was a tie that was too short to reach the waist, so the end dangled unceremoniously! This fun bag features the diagonal stripes of traditional school or formal ties, with the characteristic pointed end.

COLOURS INCORPORATED

MATERIALS

- ❖ *200g chunky-weight pure wool in main colour (M)*
- ❖ *100g chunky-weight pure wool in contrast 1 (C1)*
- ❖ *100–200g chunky-weight pure wool in contrast 2 (C2)*
- ❖ *A pair of 8mm straight needles (US11:UK0)*
- ❖ *A pair of 6.5mm double-pointed needles (US10.5:UK3)*
- ❖ *Contrast yarn to mark rows*
- ❖ *Wool needle to join seams and finish off ends of yarn*

Note: our main bag was made using Debbie Bliss Donegal Chunky Tweed in shades 292124 (M), 292123 (C1) and 292109 (C2). The variation was made using Twilley's Freedom Wool in Pewter 429 (M), Claret 412 (C1) and Damask Pink 426 (C2).

DIMENSIONS

BEFORE FELTING

Ⓦ 15¼in (38.5cm) Max Ⓗ 18¾in (47.5cm)

❖

AFTER FELTING

Ⓦ 11¼in (28.5cm) Max Ⓗ 12½in (32cm)

DIFFICULTY RATING ✚ ✚

SPECIAL TECHNIQUES
Garter stitch *see page 145*
Using stitch markers *see page 147*

Making an I-cord *see page 150*

Felting *see page 152*

ABBREVIATION
m1: *make 1 stitch by picking up the loop lying between the last and next stitch and knitting into the back of it.*

INSTRUCTIONS

The striped garter-stitch pattern in this bag is worked throughout until the upper band is reached, using 4 rows in C1, 2 rows in C2, then 6 rows in M.

The bag

Using the 8mm straight needles and C1, cast on 28 sts. Mark the end of the first row when knitted. This will show the point at the bottom of the bag which is important for alignment later. Work the increase shaping below until there are 33 sts on the needle:

Increase shaping

Row 1: Knit all stitches.
Rows 2, 3 and 4: Knit to last stitch, m1, k1.
Change to C2.
Row 5: As row 1.
Row 6: K1, m1, knit to last stitch, m1, k1 (two increases).
Change to M and repeat rows 1 to 6, all in M.

Repeat these 12 rows twice more (58 sts) and mark each end of the last row with contrast yarn. This will help when you sew the front and back together later on.

Continuing the 12-row striped pattern, work the decrease shaping as below until there are 44 sts on the needle:

Decrease shaping

Rows 1, 3, 7 and 9: K1, k2tog, knit to end.
Rows 2, 4, 6, 8 and 10: K1, k2tog, knit to last 3 sts, k2tog, k1.
Row 5: Knit all stitches.

Repeat the last 10 rows twice, then rows 1 to 9 once more (4 sts).
Next row: K2tog twice.
Next row: K2tog and fasten off.

Upper-edge band

With right side facing, turn work so the marker indicating the point of the bag is at the bottom. Using M, pick up and knit 40 sts from the side opposite the point. The stripes will now appear angled.

Knit 5 rows M, 4 rows C1, 2 rows C2 and 4 rows M.

Eyelet row: Still using M, k3, cast off 2 sts, knit to last 5 sts, cast off 2 sts, knit to end.
Next row: Knit, casting on 2 sts over each cast-off section.
Using C2, knit 2 rows, then cast off all stitches.

Work a second identical piece.

Making up

Pin the front and back together matching at each of the corners. At this stage adjacent sides will be slightly different lengths, so ease the longer edge to fit the shorter edge. This discrepancy will disappear when the bag is felted. Join four of the five sides, leaving the top of the upper-edge band open.

The handle

Using C2 and the 6.5mm double-pointed needles, cast on 5 sts and work in I-cord for 63in (160cm). Mark a point 8in (20cm) from each end of the cord. Pass the cord through one pair of adjacent eyelets and sew the end firmly to the nearest marker. Repeat with the other end of the cord and opposite pair of eyelets, to form a loose loop at each end of the handle, attached to the bag through the eyelets.

Remove the contrast markers and finish off all ends of yarn by weaving into the work before felting.

FELTING

Felt the bag in the washing machine. Our main bag felted sufficiently with three 140°F (60°C) washes and the variation with a single 140°F (60°C) wash. As you will need to pull into shape between each wash cycle, do not felt the bag too quickly (using a higher temperature) or you won't be able to reshape effectively.

VARIATION
Colours incorporated

FISHTAIL

Hans Christian Andersen's fairytale *The Little Mermaid* features six fishy-tailed sisters who rise from the bottom of the ocean to gaze at the earth as a birthday treat. Mermaids, a favourite subject of Pre-Raphaelite artists, are often portrayed holding a comb and mirror. Use this bag to carry yours while you seek out a favourite rock from which to watch the world go by.

COLOURS INCORPORATED

MATERIALS

- ❖ *50g each of four colours DK-weight pure wool*
- ❖ *A pair of 4.5mm straight needles (US7:UK7)*
- ❖ *A pair of 4.5mm double-pointed needles (US7:UK7)*
- ❖ *2 stitch markers*
- ❖ *2 stitch holders*
- ❖ *3 safety pins*
- ❖ *Wool needle to finish off ends of yarn*
- ❖ *Magnetic clasp (optional)*

Note: our main bag is made using Sheepfold's heather range DK in Loganberry, Indigo, Wisteria and Forget-me-not. The variation is made using Sirdar Eco Wool DK, shades 200, 201, 202 and 203.

DIMENSIONS

BEFORE FELTING

W 9in (23cm) **H** to lowest point (in centre)
9¾in (24.5cm) **H** to highest point (at side)
17¼in (44cm)

❖

AFTER FELTING

W 7in (18cm) **H** to lowest point (in centre) 7½in
(19cm) **H** to highest point (at side) 13in (33cm)

DIFFICULTY RATING ✜ ✜

SPECIAL TECHNIQUES

Garter stitch *see page 145*
Using stitch markers *see page 147*

Making an I-cord *see page 150*
Grafting stitches *see page 151*

Felting *see page 152*

ABBREVIATION

mfB: *knit into the front and back of the next stitch, so making 1 additional stitch.*

INSTRUCTIONS

Using the 4.5mm straight needles, cast on 3 sts in a colour of your choice.

Row 1: Knit (3 sts).

Row 2: MfB, k1, mfB (5 sts).

Row 3: K1, mfB, place marker, k1, place marker, mfB, k1 (7 sts).

Row 4: Change colour. K to first stitch before marker, mfB, slip marker across, k1, slip marker across, mfB, k to end.

Row 5: Using the same colour, repeat row 4.

Row 6: Change colour. Repeat row 4.

Rows 5 and 6 form the pattern. Continue to change colour every 2 rows introducing new colours as desired (randomly in our examples), and increasing sts in the same way until there are 87 sts. Place a thread to mark the corners at each end of the last row. There will now be 21 x 2-row stripes.

Next row: K2tog, k to first stitch before marker, mfB, slip marker across, k1, slip marker across, mfB, k to last 2 sts, k2tog (87 sts).

Continue decreasing at the side and increasing in the centre until 40 rows have been worked since placing the corner markers (a further 20 x 2-row stripes). Leave loose loops of yarn at the side edge when changing colours. These will be caught in the seam when the pieces are joined.

The upper edge

Next row: Cast off 36 sts. Knit to end of row, removing the markers.

Next row: Cast off 36 sts. Knit to end of row (15 sts remaining on the needle). Place these on a stitch holder.

Work a second side to match, again randomizing the colour changes.

Making up

Fold each side along the central increases to make the side edges of the bag and join the centre front and back seams, catching in all the loops. Sew the base seam, matching the markers. Remove markers after the seams are sewn.

The handle

Transfer the first 5 sts from one of the stitch holders to a double-pointed needle. Using a colour of your choice, work in I-cord for 27½in (70cm). Transfer these stitches to a safety pin.

Transfer the second group of 5 sts from the stitch holder to a double-pointed needle and knit a second I-cord, using a second colour. Transfer these stitches to a second safety pin.

Transfer the last group of 5 sts from the stitch holder to a double-pointed needle and knit a third I-cord, using a third colour. Transfer these stitches to a third safety pin.

You will now have three I-cords, each in a different colour, and each ending with the stitches on a safety pin. Plait these three cords together so the ends match up. Graft all 15 stitches to the 15 sts on the second stitch holder, without twisting the handle. It may be easier to transfer the 3 sets of 5 sts to a single needle before grafting.

Finish off all ends of yarn by weaving into the work before felting.

FELTING

Felt the bag in the washing machine. Our main bag felted sufficiently with two 140°F (60°C) washes and the variation with one 140°F (60°C) wash.

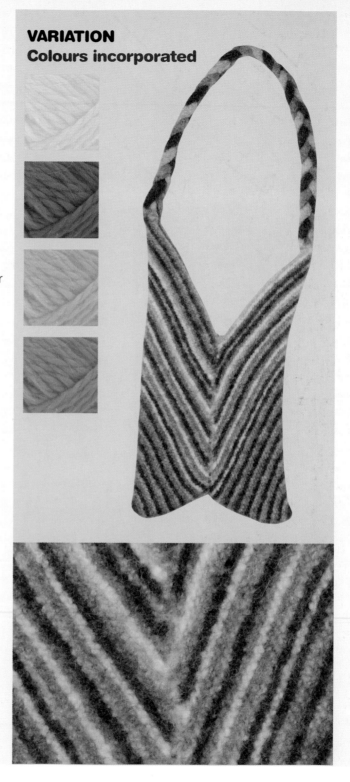

VARIATION
Colours incorporated

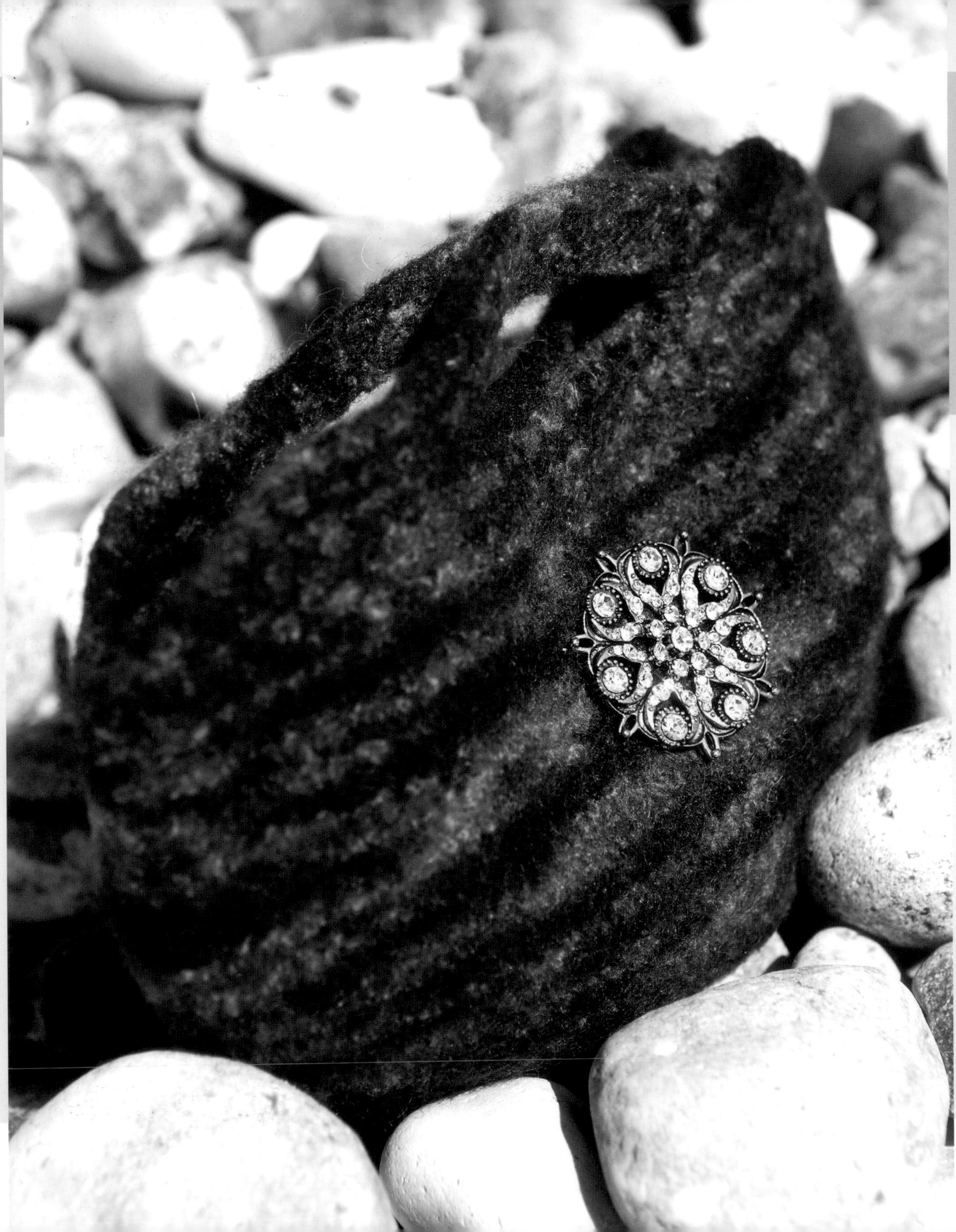

PEBBLE

There is something very comforting about holding a small round pebble, or even a worry bead, in your hand. This small clutch bag is large enough to be practical so it will not fit in your hand – but it will give you a good feeling nonetheless. Why not decorate the finished bag with pretty buttons, or even add a bit of bling!

COLOURS INCORPORATED

MATERIALS

❖ 100g aran-weight pure wool

❖ A pair of 5.5mm straight needles (US9:UK5)

❖ Wool needle to sew seams and finish off ends of yarn

❖ Magnetic clasp (optional)

❖ Brooch or buttons for decoration (optional)

Note: our main bag is made using Colinette's Iona, shade summer berries. The variation is made using a natural-coloured sheep breed wool.

DIMENSIONS

BEFORE FELTING
Ⓦ 11½in (29cm) Ⓓ 3¼in (8.5cm)
Ⓗ 9in (23cm)

❖

AFTER FELTING
Ⓦ 10¼in (26cm) Ⓓ 3in (7.5cm)
Ⓗ 6½in (16.5cm)

DIFFICULTY RATING ⊞

SPECIAL TECHNIQUES
Moss stitch *see page 145* **Garter stitch** *see page 145* **Felting** *see page 152*
Stocking stitch *see page 145*

ABBREVIATIONS
m1: *make 1 stitch by knitting into the back of the loop between the 2 stitches.*

INSTRUCTIONS
Take care to keep the moss-stitch pattern correct when shaping.

The sides
Using the 5.5mm straight needles, cast on 33 sts. Starting with a knit row and working in stocking stitch, shape the sides by increasing at each end of rows 3, 5, 7, 9, 13, 17 and 21.

Keeping the sides straight continue in stocking stitch until 28 rows have been worked (47 sts) from the cast-on edge.
Continue in stocking stitch and decrease at both ends of rows 29, 33 and 37.
Change to moss stitch (k1, p1) and, keeping the pattern correct, continue shaping.

Row 41: Work in moss stitch, decreasing at both ends.
Row 42: Work without further shaping.
Row 43 (handle opening): K2tog, work 9 sts in pattern, cast off 17 sts, work to last 2 sts, k2tog.
Row 44: Work 9 sts in pattern, cast on 17 sts, pattern to end of row.

Continue in moss stitch and shape as before by decreasing at both ends of rows 45 and 47. Cast off in moss stitch.

Work a second side to match.

The base
Using the 5.5mm straight needles, cast on 3 sts. Knit 2 rows in garter stitch.
Next row: K1, m1, k1, m1, k1 (5 sts).
Knit 3 rows.
Next row: K1, m1, k3, m1, k1 (7 sts).
Knit 5 rows.
Next row: K1, m1, k5, m1, k1 (9 sts).
Knit 5 rows.
Next row: K1, m1, k7, m1, k1 (11 sts).
Knit 5 rows.
Next row: K1, m1, k9, m1, k1 (13 sts).
Knit 6 rows.
Next row: K2tog, k to last 2 sts, k2tog (11 sts).
Knit 5 rows.

Next row: K2tog, k to last 2 sts, k2tog (9 sts).
Knit 5 rows.

Next row: K2tog, k to last 2 sts, k2tog (7 sts).
Knit 5 rows.

Next row: K2tog, k to last 2 sts, k2tog (5 sts).
Knit 3 rows.

Next row: K2tog, k1, k2tog (3 sts).
Knit 2 rows. Cast off all stitches.

Making up

Sew the cast-on edge of one side to a long side of the
base. Repeat on the other side of the base, making
sure the two sides meet at the narrow ends of the base.
Join the side seams.

FELTING

Felt the bag in the washing machine. Our main bag
felted sufficiently with a single wash at 140°F (60°C).
The variation needed three washes at 140°F (60°C)
to felt sufficiently.

Decoration

If you wish, attach a brooch or buttons to the front
before use. This is especially fun if using as an
evening bag.

VARIATION
Colours incorporated

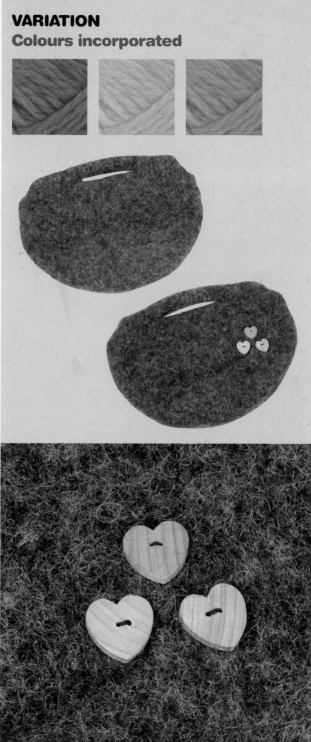

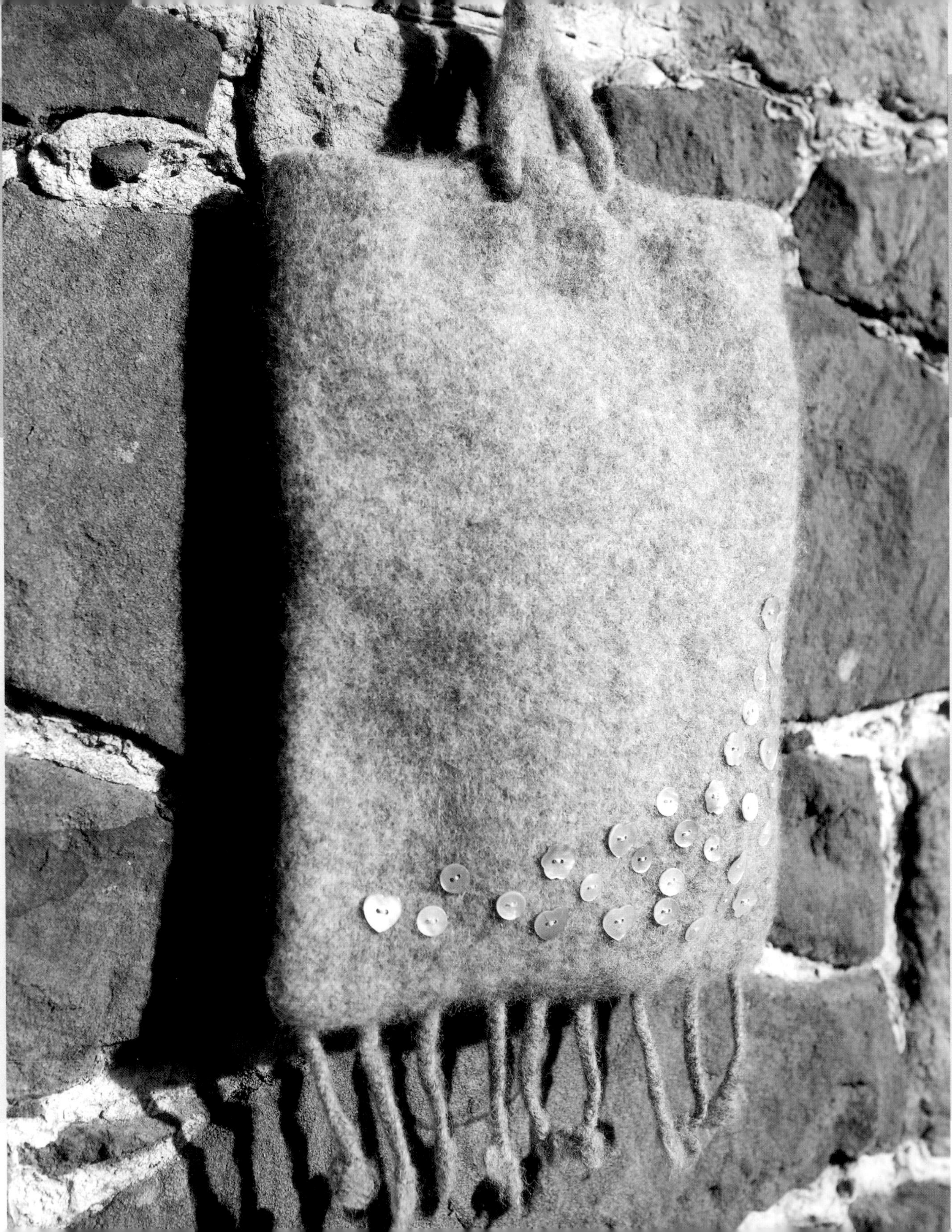

FRINGE BENEFITS

Scarves and shawls have been adorned with fringes for centuries, but they can also be used to give a bag a modern twist. Simple fringing made from plaited lengths of wool is attached before felting. Optional buttons add a quirky touch.

COLOURS INCORPORATED

MATERIALS

❖ *200g aran-weight pure wool*

❖ *A 5.5mm circular needle (US9:UK5)*

❖ *A pair of 4.5mm double-pointed needles (US7:UK7)*

❖ *4 stitch markers*

❖ *Small amount of contrast yarn to mark edges/corners*

❖ *Wool needle to finish off ends of yarn*

❖ *Magnetic clasp (optional)*

❖ *Assorted buttons for decoration (optional)*

Note: the example used 30 shell buttons in different shapes and sizes.

DIMENSIONS

BEFORE FELTING

Ⓦ 12¼in (31cm) Ⓗ 18¼in (46.5cm)

❖

AFTER FELTING

Ⓦ 8¾in (22.5cm) Ⓗ 11¾in (30cm)

DIFFICULTY RATING ⊕

SPECIAL TECHNIQUES
Garter stitch *see page 145*
Stocking stitch *see page 145*
Using stitch markers *see page 147*

Working in the round *see pages 148–9*
Making an I-cord *see page 150*
Felting *see page 152*

Attaching a magnetic clasp *see page 155*
Making a plaited fringe *instructions below*

INSTRUCTIONS

This bag is worked in the round using a circular needle.

The lower edge

Using the 5.5mm circular needle, cast on 100 sts. Knit the first row joining into a circle and taking care not to twist the stitches. Place a marker every 25 sts, using a different colour marker to indicate the start of the round. These will move up the work as you knit. Place additional markers in the lower edge, in the same position as the stitch markers. These will remain in place, and will help to align the piece when the lower edge is joined. Purl 1 round, knit 1 round, purl 1 round to form the garter-stitch lower edge.

The body

Knit 100 rounds ending at the marker indicating the start of the round. At this point the work will measure approximately 17in (43cm).

The upper edge

Purl 1 round, slipping the markers as before.

Next round: *Knit 4 sts. Cast off 4 sts. Knit to next marker. Slip the marker. Knit to 8 sts before the next marker. Cast off 4 sts. Knit to next marker. Slip the marker**. Repeat * to ** once more.

Purl 1 round, knit 1 round, purl 1 round, knit 1 round to form the garter-stitch upper edge. Cast off all stitches.

Making up

Fold the bag so that the edge markers match up and the holes for the handle are in the centre of the top edges. Sew the lower edge together.

The handle

Using the 4.5mm double-pointed needles, cast on 5 sts and work in I-cord for 59in (150cm). Mark a point 8in (20cm) from each end of the cord. Pass the I-cord through one pair of eyelet holes and sew the end of the cord firmly to the adjacent marker. Repeat with the other end of the I-cord and the opposite pair of eyelet holes, forming a loose loop at each end of the handle, attached to the bag through the eyelet holes.

Finish off all ends of yarn by weaving into the work before felting.

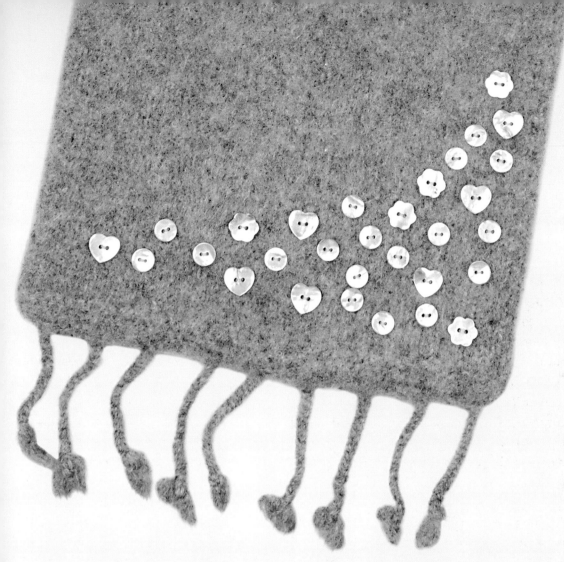

The plaited fringing

Cut three 12in (30cm) lengths of yarn and sew each through a single point on the lower edge of the bag. Divide the six resulting lengths of yarn into three pairs, taking a strand from either side of the edge. Plait, then knot the end to secure. Repeat using identical bundles of yarn along the base of the bag. Our example used nine evenly spaced bundles of plaited yarn.

FELTING

Felt the bag in the washing machine. Our example felted sufficiently with two 140°F (60°C) washes.

Decoration (optional)

Sew a selection of buttons to the front of your bag.

Attaching a clasp (optional)

If you want additional security for your bag, fasten a magnetic clasp centrally to either side of the inside upper edge of the bag.

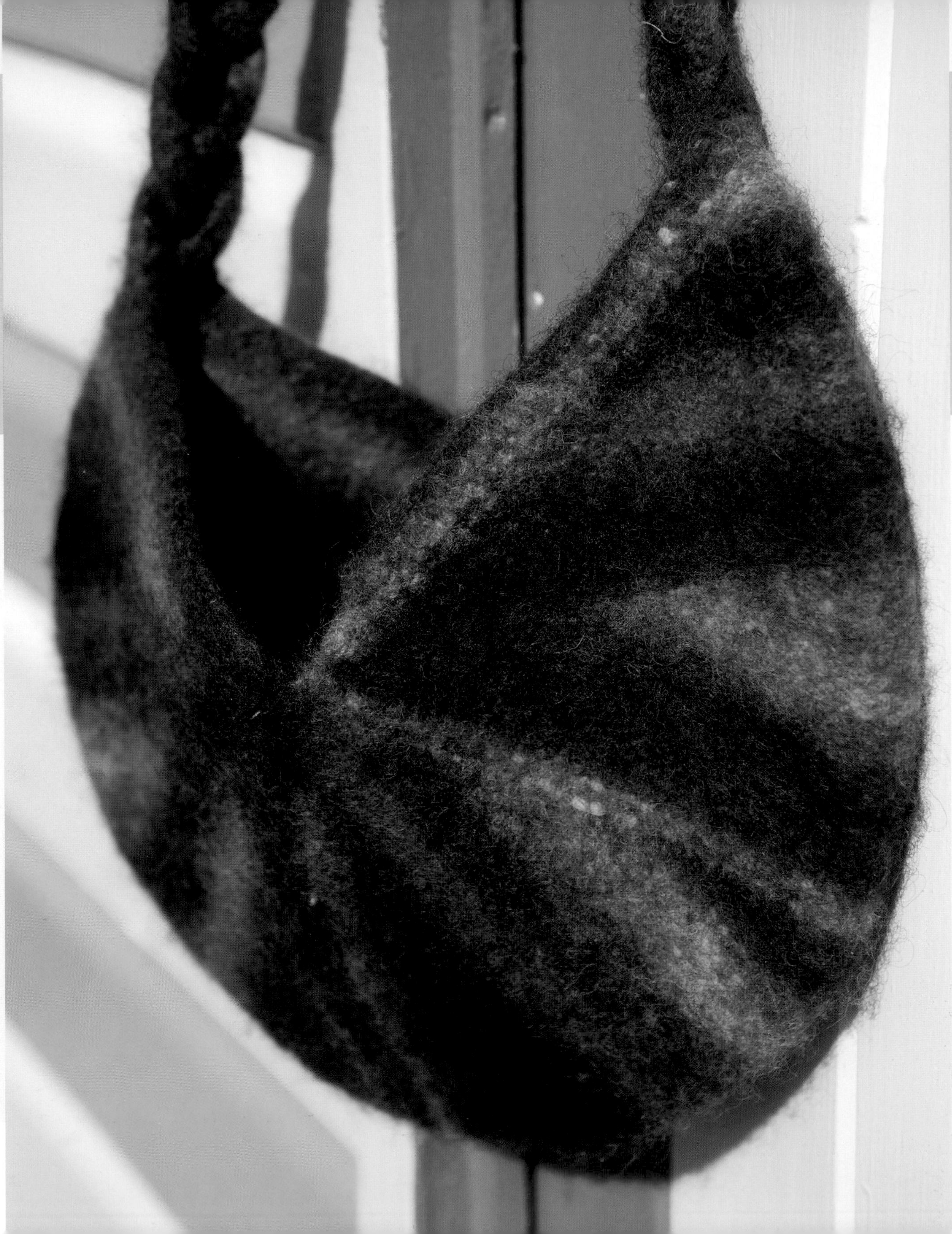

ORANGE SEGMENTS

Cut a juicy orange in half and then marvel at its fabulous segmented design before succumbing to the temptation to eat it. This bag has the same rounded shape as a citrus fruit and visualization of the segments is enhanced if you use a multi-coloured yarn. The brighter the better if you want your bag to stand out in a crowd.

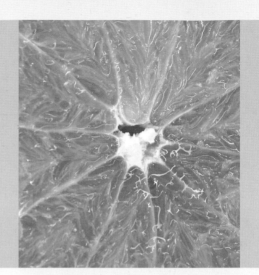

COLOURS INCORPORATED

MATERIALS

- ❖ *150g aran-weight pure wool*
- ❖ *A pair of 5.5mm straight needles (US9:UK5)*
- ❖ *A pair of 4.5mm double-pointed needles US7:UK7)*
- ❖ *4 stitch markers made from contrast yarn*
- ❖ *3 safety pins or stitch holders*
- ❖ *Wool needle to graft handle and finish off ends of yarn*

Note: our main bag was made using Noro Kureyon, shade 208 and the variation using Noro Kureyon, shade 156.

DIMENSIONS

BEFORE FELTING

Max **W** 16½in (42cm)

H to centre 9¼in (23.5cm)

H to side 14¾in (37.5cm)

❖

AFTER FELTING

Max **W** 12¼in (31cm) **H** to centre 6¾in (17cm) **H** to side 9¾in (24.5cm)

DIFFICULTY RATING ✪ ✪ ✪

SPECIAL TECHNIQUES

Garter stitch *see page 145*   **Using stitch markers** *see page 147*   **Felting** *see page 152*
Stocking stitch *see page 145*   **Making an I-cord** *see page 150*

INSTRUCTIONS

Segments

Using the 5.5mm straight needles, cast on 65 sts. Knit 30 sts, place a marker made from your contrast yarn, knit 5 sts, place a second marker, knit to end.
Note: the two markers should now indicate the centre 5 sts of the piece and remain in place; do not try to move them as you knit!

Row 1: K2tog, knit to last 2 sts, k2tog.
Repeat row 1 three times more to provide a garter stitch edge.

Next row (row 2): P2tog, purl to last 2 sts, p2tog.
Repeat rows 1 and 2 until 5 sts remain, so making a decreasing stocking-stitch panel.

*Pick up and work 30 sts from the adjacent sloping edge. Turn work and, continuing in stocking stitch, work the 35 sts on your needle. Pick up and work 30 more sts from the second sloping edge (65 sts).

Decrease by repeating rows 1 and 2 on these 65 sts until 5 sts remain on your needle, as before**.

Repeat from * to **, until you have worked a total of seven panels. Pick up the two lots of 30 sts as before and repeat row 1 four times to give a garter-stitch edge. Cast off all stitches, placing markers either end of the centre 5 sts, made from your contrast yarn.

The handle

Using the 4.5mm double-pointed needles, pick up and knit the 5 centre stitches on the cast-on edge (5 sts). Work in I-cord on these stitches for 27½in (70cm). Place stitches on a safety pin or stitch holder.

Pick up and knit the 5 sts to one side of the first I-cord and knit an identical length cord. Pick up and knit the 5 sts to the other side of the first I-cord and knit a third identical-length cord. Plait the three I-cords together and sew to the opposite side of the bag, using the marker threads to assist in positioning.

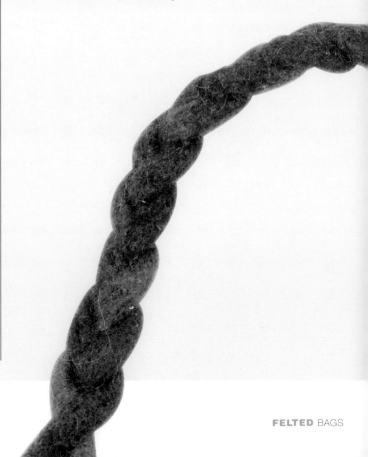

Making up

Remove the four markers indicating handle position.

Join the garter-stitch borders where they meet at the middle of the bag, on both front and back.

Finish off all ends of yarn by weaving into the work before felting.

FELTING

Felt the bag in the washing machine. Our examples felted sufficiently with two 140°F (60°C) washes.

VARIATION
Colours incorporated

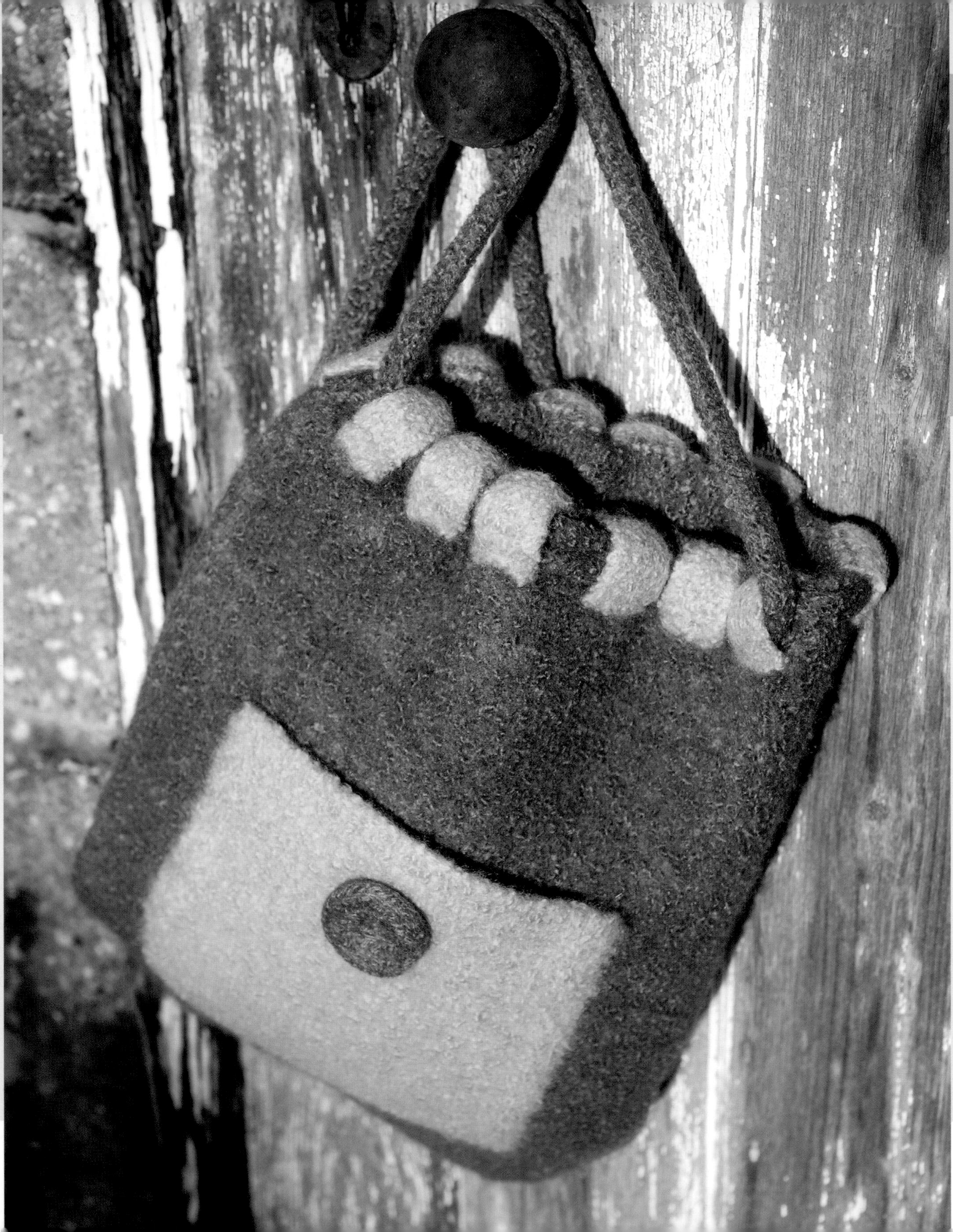

SHOE BAG

Starting school is a special time. Remember walking into the cloakroom to find your peg? Who was more anxious, parent or child? Brightly coloured shoe bags hanging on rows of wooden pegs can be a reassuring sight, and this design recreates their simple drawstring style, with a buttoned front pocket. Use this felted bag for shoes, lunches or notebook and pens – it's up to you.

COLOURS INCORPORATED

MATERIALS

❖ *300g aran-weight pure wool in darker shade (M)*

❖ *100g aran-weight pure wool in paler shade (C)*

❖ *A pair of 5.5mm straight needles (US9:UK5)*

❖ *A pair of 4.5mm double-ended needles (US7:UK7)*

❖ *Wool needle to join bag pieces and finish off ends of yarn*

Note: our examples were made using Texere's Airedale Aran. The main bag is in shades Dusky Lavender (M) and Dusky Lilac (C). The variation is in shades indigo (M) and denim (C).

DIMENSIONS

BEFORE FELTING

W 14½in (37cm) **H** 22in (56cm)

❖

AFTER FELTING

W 10½in (26.5cm) **H** 12¾in (32.5cm)

DIFFICULTY RATING ✦ ✦

SPECIAL TECHNIQUES
Stocking stitch *see page 145*   **Making an I-cord** *see page 150*   **Felting** *see page 152*
Garter stitch *see page 145*

INSTRUCTIONS

This bag is worked on straight needles in stocking stitch with garter-stitch edges.

The side

Using the 5.5mm straight needles and M, cast on 60 sts and knit 4 rows to form a garter-stitch edge.

Stocking-stitch pattern with garter-stitch edges:
Row 1: Knit 1 row.
Row 2: K3, purl to last 3 stitches, k3.

Repeat rows 1 and 2 until a total of 122 rows have been worked from the cast-on edge. This will give a stocking-stitch piece with garter-stitch side edges. At this point the height of the bag will be approximately 21¼in (54cm).

Knit 2 rows to form a garter-stitch fold line at the base of your bag. Work a further 118 rows in the stocking-stitch pattern with garter-stitch edges as above. Knit 5 rows to form a final garter stitch edge, then cast off all stitches.

Fold the bag in half along the garter-stitch fold line and sew the side seams together.

Upper-edge tabs

Using the 5.5mm straight needles and C, pick up and knit 5 sts from those forming the cast-on edge, starting at one of the side seams. Knit 12 rows, then cast off all stitches. Miss 5 sts along the cast-on edge, then pick up and knit the next 5 sts as before. Make an identical tab and cast off all stitches. Continue in this way round the top edge of the bag to create a total of 12 tabs with a 5-st gap between each.

Fold each tab down over the outside of the bag and sew each to the body of the bag along the narrow edge of the tabs. There should now be a series of loops through which to thread the handle when felted.

Corner tabs at base

Using the 5.5mm straight needles and C cast on 12 sts.
Row 1: Knit all stitches.
Rows 2 and 3: K2tog, knit to end.
Row 4: K2tog, k2, cast off 3 sts, knit to end.
Row 5: K2tog, k1, cast on 3sts over sts previously cast off, knit to end.

Repeat rows 2 and 3 until only 2 sts remain. K2tog and fasten off yarn.
Work a second identical corner tab.

Sew the cast-on edge of one tab to one of the side seams, aligning the corner of the tab to the corner at the base of the bag. Repeat on the other side with the second tab.

The pocket

Using the 5.5mm straight needles and C, cast on 35 sts and knit 4 rows. Work the stocking-stitch pattern with garter-stitch side edges as above until 46 rows have been worked from the cast-on edge.

Next row (buttonhole): K13, cast off 9, knit to end.
Next row: Work in pattern, casting on 9 sts over the cast-off stitches.

Work 8 more rows in pattern, then knit 5 rows to give a garter-stitch upper edge. Cast off all stitches.

Making up

Place the pocket on your bag with the pocket base approximately 20 rows up from the bag base and the sides of the pockets approximately 12 sts in from the sides of the bag. Sew securely in place along the two side edges and the base edge.

Making the button

Using the 4.5mm double-pointed needles and M, cast on 3 sts. Work in I-cord on these stitches for 10in (25cm). Cast off all stitches. Coil the cord into a loose spiral and sew together securely, taking care to keep the round button flat.

The handle

Using the 4.5mm double-pointed needles and M, cast on 5 sts and work in I-cord for 90½in (230cm). Cast off all stitches.

Finish off all ends of yarn by weaving into the work before felting.

FELTING

Felt the pieces in the washing machine. We recommend felting the button, handle and bag separately. Our examples felted sufficiently with one 140°F (60°C) wash. Leave the pieces to dry.

Finishing

To insert the handle, lay the bag flat, pocket uppermost. Thread the handle through all the tabs around the upper edge, then again through the tabs on the front of the bag to create a drawstring effect, closing the bag when the handle is pulled. Pass the ends of the handle through the holes in the tabs at the lower corners of the bag and knot securely, making sure the knot is too big to pass back through the hole.

Attach the felted button to the front of the bag, aligning with the buttonhole in the pocket.

VARIATION
Colours incorporated

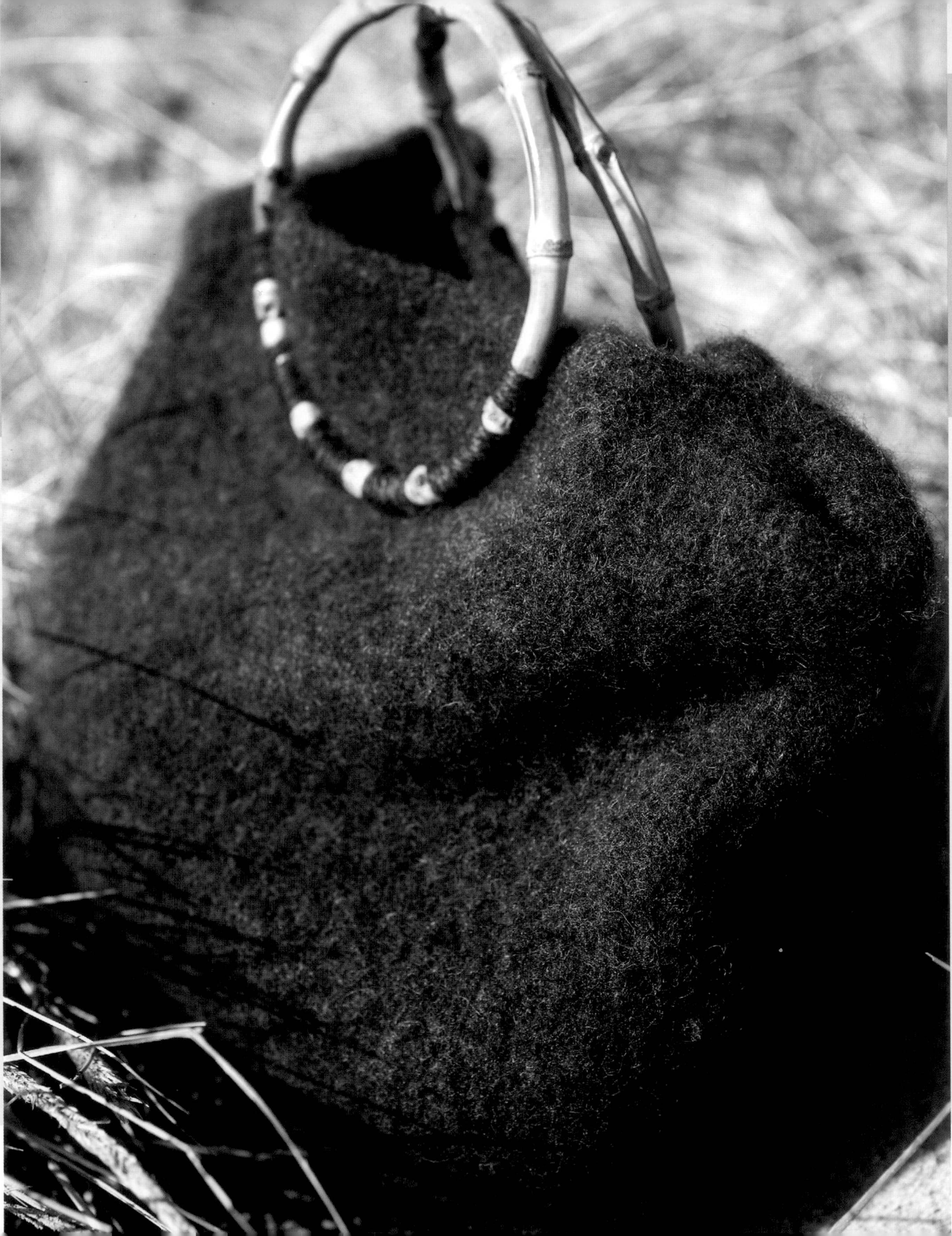

SEASIDE

Trips to the beach laden with towels, bathing suits, buckets, spades and sandwiches are a wonderful memory of childhood holidays. The picnic was carried in a straw bag with big round handles that were ideal for tying on bits and pieces, including dangling, salty seaweed! This design is inspired by that straw bag, which was brought out year after year.

COLOURS INCORPORATED

MATERIALS

❖ *400g aran-weight pure wool*

❖ *A pair of 5.5mm straight needles (US9:UK5)*

❖ *A 5.5mm circular needle (US9:UK5)*

❖ *4 stitch markers*

❖ *Small amount of contrast yarn to mark the upper edge of the bag*

❖ *Wool needle to join the bag and finish off ends of yarn*

❖ *A pair of circular bag handles approximately 6in (15cm) in diameter*

Note: the main bag was made using Sheepfold's Heather range in blueberry and the variation using British Breeds' Manx Loghtan wool. The examples use Creative Naturals handbag handles by Blumenthal Craft: 90-00-18947 for the main bag and 90-00-18950 for the variation.

DIMENSIONS

BEFORE FELTING

Ⓦ 15in (38cm) Ⓓ 5½in (14cm)

Ⓗ 17¾in (45cm)

AFTER FELTING

Ⓦ 11½in (29cm) Ⓓ 4½in (11.5cm)

Ⓗ 11½in (29cm)

DIFFICULTY RATING ✦ ✦

INSTRUCTIONS

This bag is knitted in the round using a circular needle.

The base

Using the 5.5mm straight needles, cast on 50 sts and knit 40 rows to form a garter-stitch base. Change to the circular needle and knit 1 row (from the straight needle), pick up and knit 28 sts along the short edge of the base, 50 sts along the second long edge and 28 sts along the second short edge, placing a stitch marker at each corner (156 sts). Use a different coloured marker to indicate the beginning/end of the round.

Knit 86 rounds, moving the markers across as they are reached, ending at the marker at the start of the round. At this point the height of your bag will be approximately 17in (43cm).

The upper edge

Purl 1 round, knit 1 round, purl 1 round. Cast off all stitches k-wise, using contrast yarn to mark the position of the stitch markers.

Making up

To encourage the sides to pleat inwards, fold the short sides inwards, matching the corner markers. Sew the upper edge together from the fold edge up to the matched corner markers.

Remove all contrast yarn markers. Finish off all ends of yarn by weaving into the work before felting.

FELTING

Felt the bag in the washing machine. Our examples felted sufficiently with two 140°F (60°C) washes.

The handle

When the bag is fully dry, place one of the handles centrally on the outside of one long side, overlapping the garter-stitch upper edge, and sew neatly in place using the aran-weight wool. Repeat on the second side, making sure the two handles are properly aligned for the best result.

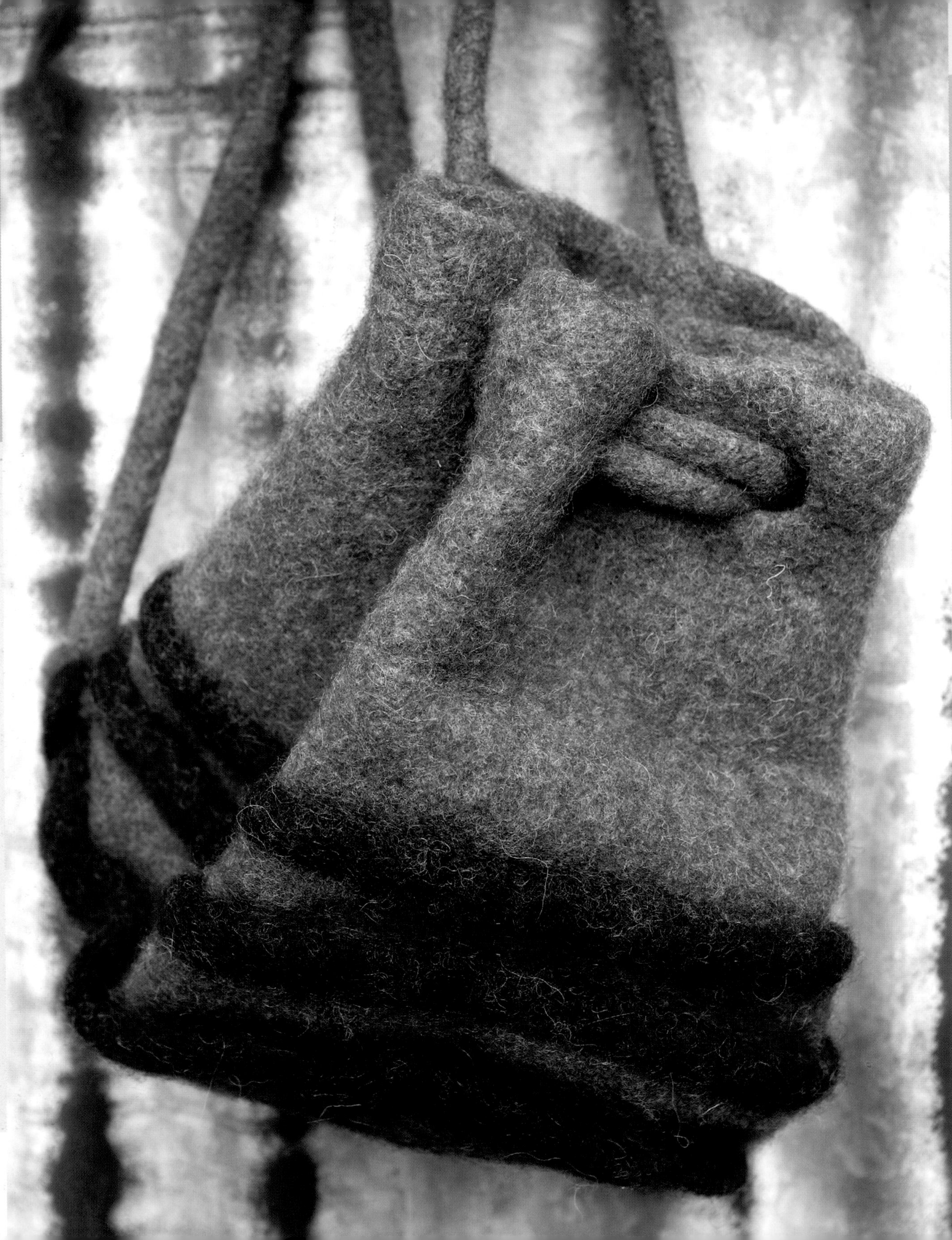

DUFFEL

Duffel bags were originally made from thick woollen cloth and named after the Belgian town where the fabric was made. Before rucksacks and backpacks became popular, scouts and guides would carry their kit for a day's hiking in these cylindrical bags with drawstring closures. Modern duffel bags are often made from polyester or nylon, but this is your chance to recreate a woollen version.

MATERIALS

- ❖ 300–400g aran-weight pure wool in main colour (M)
- ❖ 100g aran-weight pure wool in contrast colour (C)
- ❖ A 5.5mm circular needle (US9:UK5)
- ❖ A set of four 5.5mm double-pointed needles (US9:UK5)
- ❖ A pair of 4.5mm double-pointed needles (US7:UK7)
- ❖ Stitch marker
- ❖ Small amount of contrast yarn to mark edges/corners
- ❖ Wool needle to finish off ends of yarn

Note: our main bag was made using British Breeds wool: 400g Manx Loghtan (M) and 100g Black Jacob (C). The variation was made using Sheepfold's aran: 300g Flint (M) and 100g pumice (C).

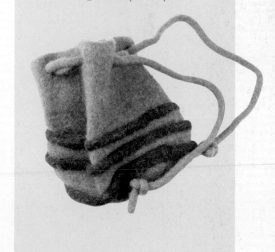

INSTRUCTIONS

This bag is worked from the top to the bottom.

The bag

Using M and the 5.5mm circular needle, cast on 128 sts. Place a stitch marker to indicate the start of the round, taking care not to twist the stitches when joining the round as you start knitting. Knit the first round ending at the marker. * Purl 1 round, knit 1 round** slipping the stitch marker as it is reached. Repeat the last 2 rounds three more times (9 rounds knitted since casting on). Knit 1 more round.

Next row (eyelets): Starting at the stitch marker, knit 6 sts. Cast off 4 sts. *Knit 11 sts (12 sts on needle), cast off 4 sts**. Repeat * to ** six times more. Knit to end of round.

Next round: Knit, casting on 4 sts over each group of 4 sts previously cast off (eight eyelets evenly spaced round the bag).

Knit 48 more rounds. At this point, the work should measure approx. 12in (30cm) from the cast-on edge.

The pleats

First pleat: Break off M and join in C. Purl 6 rounds. Break off C and rejoin M. Fold rows worked in C and, in the next round, knit the stitch on the needle together with the loop at the back of the last row knitted in M before the C pleat.
Knit 13 rounds in M.

Second pleat: Break off M and join in C. Purl 8 rounds. Break off C and rejoin M. Form a pleat, as before. Knit 13 rounds in M.

Third pleat: Break off M and join in C. Purl 10 rounds. Break off C and rejoin M. Form a pleat, as before.

Knit 1 round in M, placing contrast yarn markers to indicate the position of the handle loops on the 16th and 112th stitches. These will be worked later.

The base

The base is worked in decreasing rounds. Change to 5.5mm double-pointed needles when it becomes too difficult to knit with the circular needle.

First round of base: *K14, k2tog**. Repeat * to ** to end of round (120 sts).
Knit 2 rounds.

Next round: *K13, k2tog**. Repeat * to ** to end of round (112 sts).
Knit 2 rounds.

Next round: Change to C and *k12, k2tog**. Repeat * to ** to end of round (104 sts). Knit 1 round.

Next round: Change to M and *k11, k2tog**. Repeat * to ** to end of round (96 sts). Knit 1 round.

Next round: *K10, k2tog**. Repeat * to ** to end of round (88 sts).
Knit 1 round.

Next round: *K9, k2tog**. Repeat * to ** to end of round (80 sts).
Knit 1 round.

Next round: Change to C and *k8, k2tog**. Repeat *
to ** to end of round (72 sts).

Knit 1 round.

Next round: Change to M and *k7, k2tog**. Repeat *
to ** to end of round (64 sts).

Knit 1 round.

Next round: *K6, k2tog**. Repeat * to ** to end of
round (56 sts).

Knit 1 round.

Next round: *K5, k2tog**. Repeat * to ** to end of
round (48 sts).

Knit 1 round.

Next round: Change to C and *k4, k2tog**. Repeat *
to ** to end of round (40 sts).

Knit 1 round.

Next round: Change to M and *k3, k2tog**. Repeat *
to ** to end of round (32 sts).

Knit 1 round.

Next round: *K2, k2tog**. Repeat * to ** to end of
round (24 sts).

Knit 1 round.

Next round: *K1, k2tog**. Repeat * to ** to end of
round (16 sts).

Knit 1 round.

Next round: *K2tog**. Repeat * to ** to end of round.
Break off yarn and draw through remaining stitches to
close the centre of the base. Fasten off securely.

The handle

Using the 4.5mm double-pointed needles, cast on 5 sts
and work in I-cord for 98in (250cm). Cast off all stitches.

Handle loops

Using C and the 4.5mm double-pointed needles, pick
up and knit 4 sts to the right of the first marked stitch
in the last row of the pleat. Work in I-cord for 15 rows,

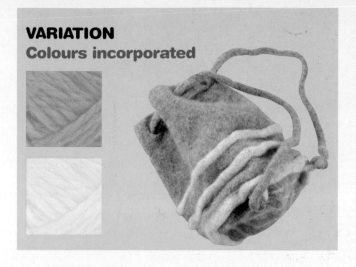

**VARIATION
Colours incorporated**

then graft to the 4 sts sitting to the left of the marked
stitch. Repeat at the second marked stitch to form a
further loop.

Finishing off

Remove all contrast yarn markers. Finish off all ends of
yarn by weaving into the work before felting.

Place the bag sitting on its base with the handle loops
facing. Starting at the eyelet above the right-hand loop,
thread the I-cord handle in and out of the eyelets around
the top of the bag, anti-clockwise. Go round a second
time to the eyelet above the left-hand loop; the handle
will have passed through the eyelets for almost two
complete rounds. The two ends of the I-cord should be
dangling on the outside of the bag.

FELTING

Felt the bag in the washing machine. Our examples
felted sufficiently with two 140°F (60°C) washes.

Finishing

When the bag is dry, knot the ends of the I-cord firmly
to the loops at the base.

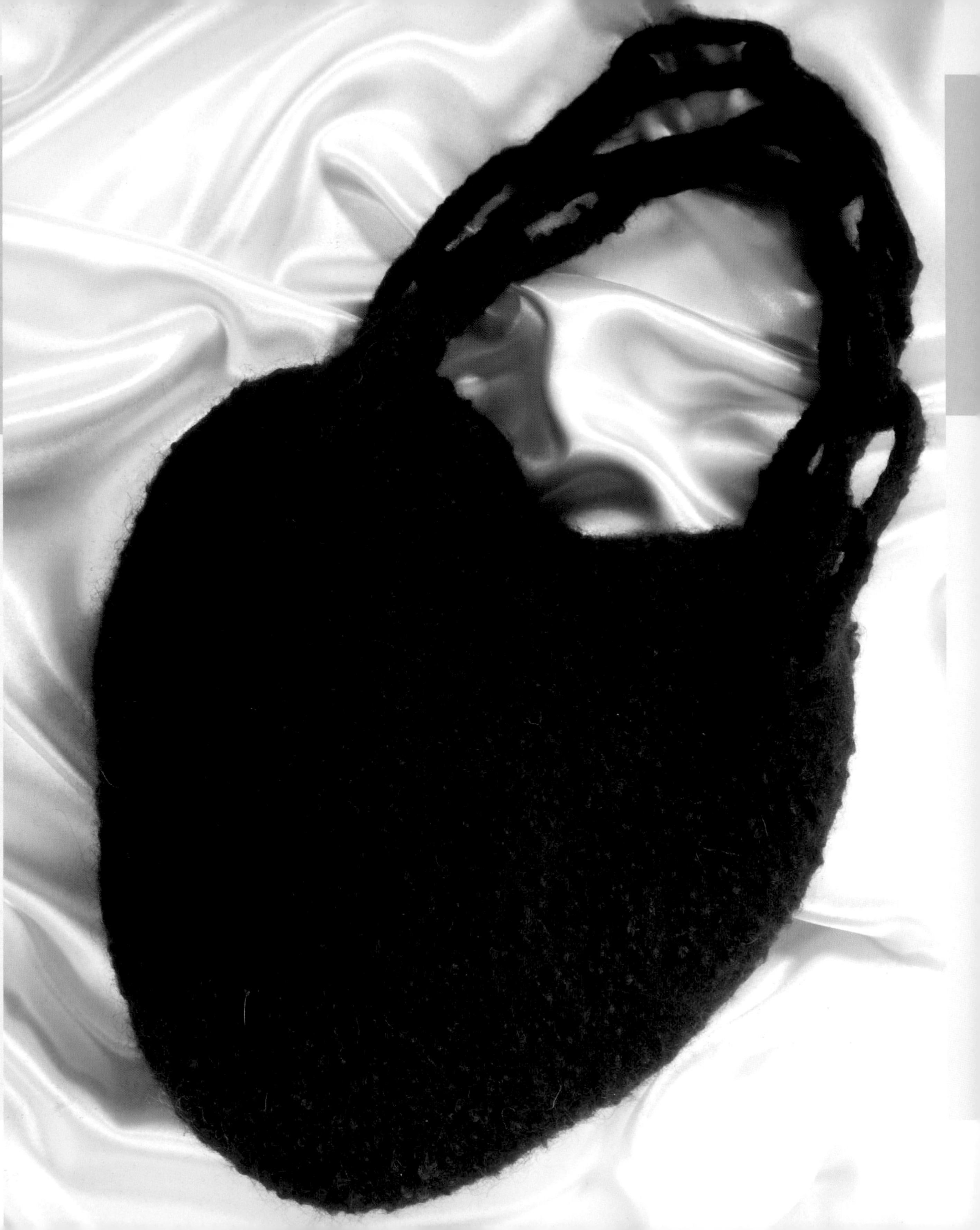

RETRO HEART

This heart-shaped bag is knitted with lustrous wool formed from the long ringlets of the Wensleydale sheep that originate from northern England. Heart shapes have long symbolized true love and were much used by the Victorians to decorate their Valentine's Day greetings. Nowadays, heart motifs are adored by children and adults alike and cover bedding, clothes, notebooks, china and more.

COLOURS INCORPORATED

MATERIALS

❖ 350g aran-weight (main bag) or 500g aran+ weight (variation)

❖ A pair of 5.5mm straight needles (US9:UK5)

❖ A pair of 4.5mm double-pointed needles (US7:UK7)

❖ Stitch holder or large safety pin

❖ Large-headed pins to fasten pieces

❖ Wool needle to sew pieces together and finish off ends of yarn

❖ 8in (20cm) zip

❖ Matching sewing thread and needle

Note: our examples were made using Wensleydale Longwool.
The main bag was made using aran in Pomegranate, the variation
using aran+ in Marshmallow.

DIMENSIONS

BEFORE FELTING
Max **W** 19¼in (49cm) **D** 6in (15cm)
Max **H** 17½in (44.5cm)

AFTER FELTING
Max **W** 11¼in (28.5cm) **D** 4in (10.5cm)
Max **H** 8½in (22cm)

DIFFICULTY RATING ✽ ✽ ✽

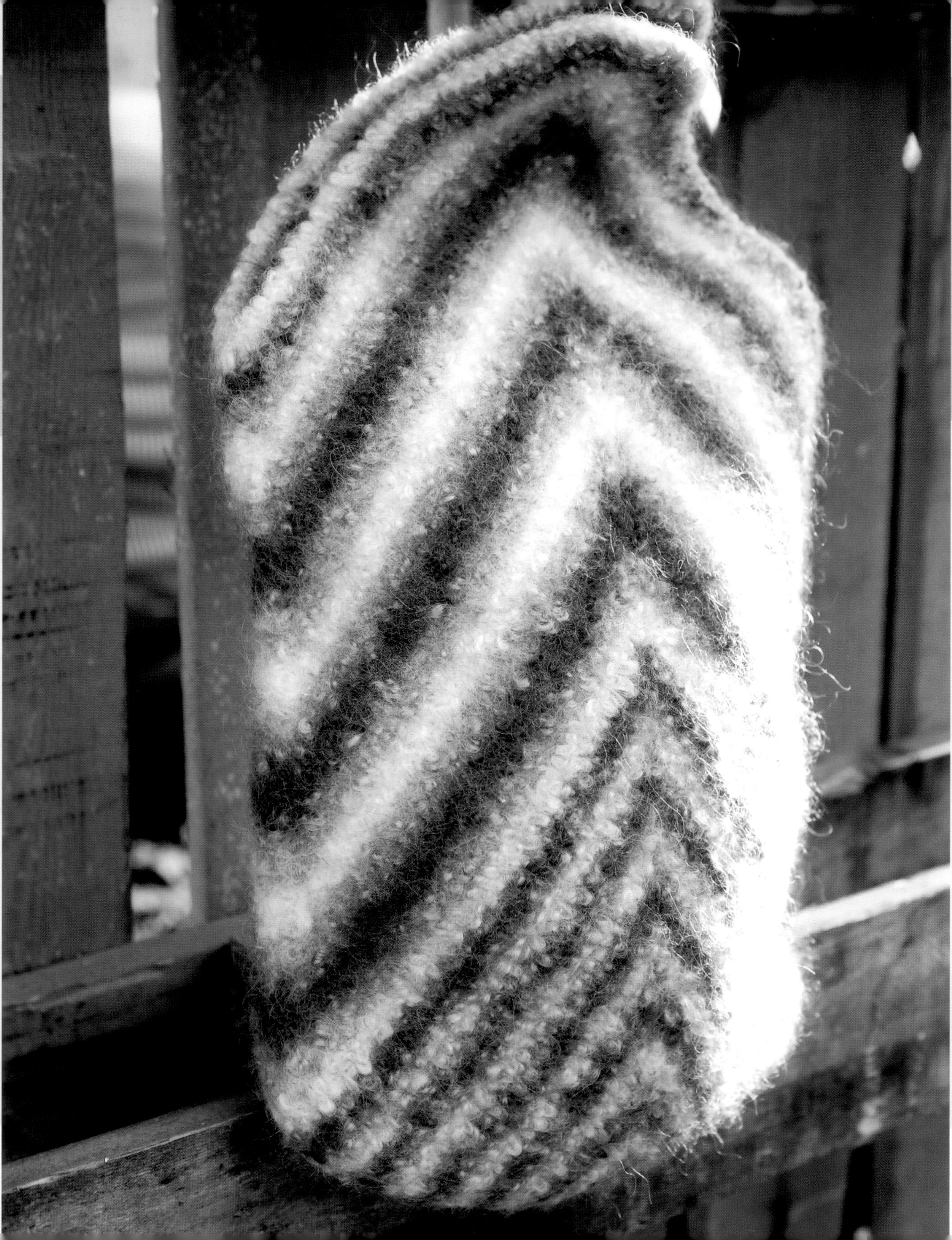

CHEVRON

The chevron has traditionally signified something important, whether status, as for a sergeant's stripes, or a warning, as in road traffic signs. V-shaped chevron stripes are the theme for this bag, ultimately knitted on a circular needle to remind us of the signs on endless roundabouts, so common in Britain. With the bag you go round and round and round, but we don't recommend that at roundabouts!

COLOURS INCORPORATED

MATERIALS

❖ 100g aran-weight pure wool in each of 4 colours (C1, C2, C3 and C4)

❖ A pair of 5.5mm straight needles (US9:UK5)

❖ A 5.5mm circular needle (US9:UK5)

❖ A pair of 4.5mm double-ended needles (US7:UK7)

❖ 8 stitch markers, preferably 4 in each of 2 colours

❖ Large stitch holder

❖ Small amount of contrast yarn to mark position of handle

❖ Wool needle to finish off ends of yarn

Note: our main bag was made using aran-weight Wensleydale Longwool in Silver Green 33 (C1), Teal 52 (C2), Fennel 02 (C3) and Natural 01 (C4). The variation was made using Jamieson's aran-weight Shetland wool in assorted natural shades.

DIMENSIONS

BEFORE FELTING

Ⓦ 14½in (37cm) Ⓗ at centre 27¾in (70.5cm)

❖

AFTER FELTING

Ⓦ 10in (25cm) Ⓗ at centre 18¾in (47.5cm)

DIFFICULTY RATING ✪ ✪ ✪

SPECIAL TECHNIQUES

Garter stitch *see page 145*
Stocking stitch *see page 145*
Using stitch markers *see page 147*

Working in the round *see page 148*
Making an I-cord *see page 150*
Grafting stitches *see page 151*

Felting *see page 152*

ABBREVIATION

mfB: *knit into the front and back of the next stitch, so making 1 additional stitch.*

INSTRUCTIONS

This bag is made with two garter-stitch triangles, joined and knitted in the round to give wider stripes thereafter. The upper edge is two points in the centre of the bag.

Note: as you will need to identify the right side of your work later, attach a safety pin near the beginning of each of the triangular shapes to mark this. It is hard to tell, just by looking, in a garter-stitch piece!

Triangular side

Using the 5.5mm straight needles and C1, cast on 3 sts and knit 1 row.

Next row: MfB, k1, mfB (5 sts).

Next row: MfB, place marker (increase marker 1), k1, place marker (increase marker 2), mfB, k1 (7 sts). Break off C1, join in C2.

Next row (increase pattern): *Knit to one stitch before first marker, mfB, slip marker across, k1, slip marker across, mfB, knit to end**.

Work one more increase pattern in C2 (2 rows in total), then two in C3 and two in C4 (19 sts). Work two increase rows in C1. This sets the colour change pattern so the colour changes every two rows (C1 to C2 to C3 to C4 to C1…). Continue in this way until there are 99 sts on the needle (you will have just completed the second row of a C4 stripe).

Transfer your work to the large stitch holder and make a second identical piece.

Central section

This second section is knitted in the round, giving the appearance of stocking stitch. With RS facing, and using C1, work one of the triangular pieces onto the 5.5mm circular needle as follows:

K1, place marker (decrease marker 1), k2tog, knit to 1 st before increase marker 1, mfB, slip marker across, k1, slip marker across, mfB, knit to last 3 sts k2tog, place marker (decrease marker 2). Knit the last st in this triangle together with the first st on the second triangle. Place marker (decrease marker 3), k2tog, knit to 1 st before increase marker (now number 3), mfB, slip marker across, k1, slip marker across (now number 4), mfB, knit to last 3 sts k2tog, place marker (decrease

marker 4). Knit the last st in this triangle together with the first st on the circular needle, so closing the loop, taking care not to twist the work when joining the two ends (196 sts).
Note: this round sets the positions of the increases and decreases that form the chevron pattern.

Next round: Using C1, ❖ *slip marker across, k2tog, knit to 1 st before increase marker, mfB, slip marker across, k1, slip marker across, mfB, knit to 2 sts before decrease marker, k2tog, slip marker across, k1**.
Repeat * to ** once to complete the round. ❖❖

Work ❖ to ❖❖ twice more in C1, then four times in C2, four times in C3 and four times in C4. This sets the 4-row-stripe chevron pattern. Continue until 10 stripes have been worked (40 rounds in total).

Keeping the order of colour change as before, with C3 work ❖ to ❖❖ once more.

Note: in the next round you will temporarily remove the first pair of increase markers, but these will be replaced in the subsequent round, so don't throw them away!

Next round: Work pattern until 2 sts before the first increase marker. Cast off 5 sts, removing the two increase markers. Continue working the chevron pattern until 4 sts before the first increase marker on the opposite side of the bag. Knit and mark the next stitch with waste yarn

to assist when placing the handle later on. Continue in the chevron pattern until 4 sts after the second increase marker. Knit and mark the next stitch with waste yarn, as before, to assist when placing the handle later. Complete the round. The cast-off section will subsequently form the eyelet hole.

Next round: Work in chevron pattern to the start of the eyelet hole. Cast on 4 sts, replace marker (*increase marker 1*), cast on 1 st, replace marker (*increase marker 2*), finally cast on 4 sts. Continue to the end of the round, shaping as in earlier rounds.

Work one more round, so completing the eleventh 4-row stripe.
Break off C3 and join in C4.

Work ❖ to ❖❖ four times, so giving a twelfth 4-row stripe.

Upper edge
Work ❖ to ❖❖ twice in C1, with the second round worked in purl, so starting the garter-stitch edge.
Now work 2 'garter stitch' rounds (knit 1 round, purl 1 round) similarly in C2, 2 in C3 and 1 in C4.
Continuing in C4, cast off all stitches p-wise.

Handle

With the WS facing, locate the first marked stitch in the eleventh 4-row stripe. Using a double-pointed needle and C3, pick up and knit 5 sts from the same round, working towards the centre of the chevron. Work in I-cord on these stitches for 25½in (65cm).

Graft the stitches to those leading from the centre to the second marked stitch, so the handle is symmetrical around the centre of the chevron. This forms a wrist loop that threads through the eyelet on the opposite side, so closing the bag.

Making up

Lie the bag flat with the points at the top of the chevron sitting centrally between the left- and right-hand edges of the bag. Line up the base seam by matching the coloured stripes and sew together. The bag will not sit totally flat at this stage, but will after felting!

Finish off all ends of yarn by weaving into the work before felting.

FELTING

Felt the bag in the washing machine. Our main bag felted sufficiently with a single 140°F (60°C) wash. The variation felted sufficiently with two 140°F (60°C) washes.

VARIATION
Colours incorporated

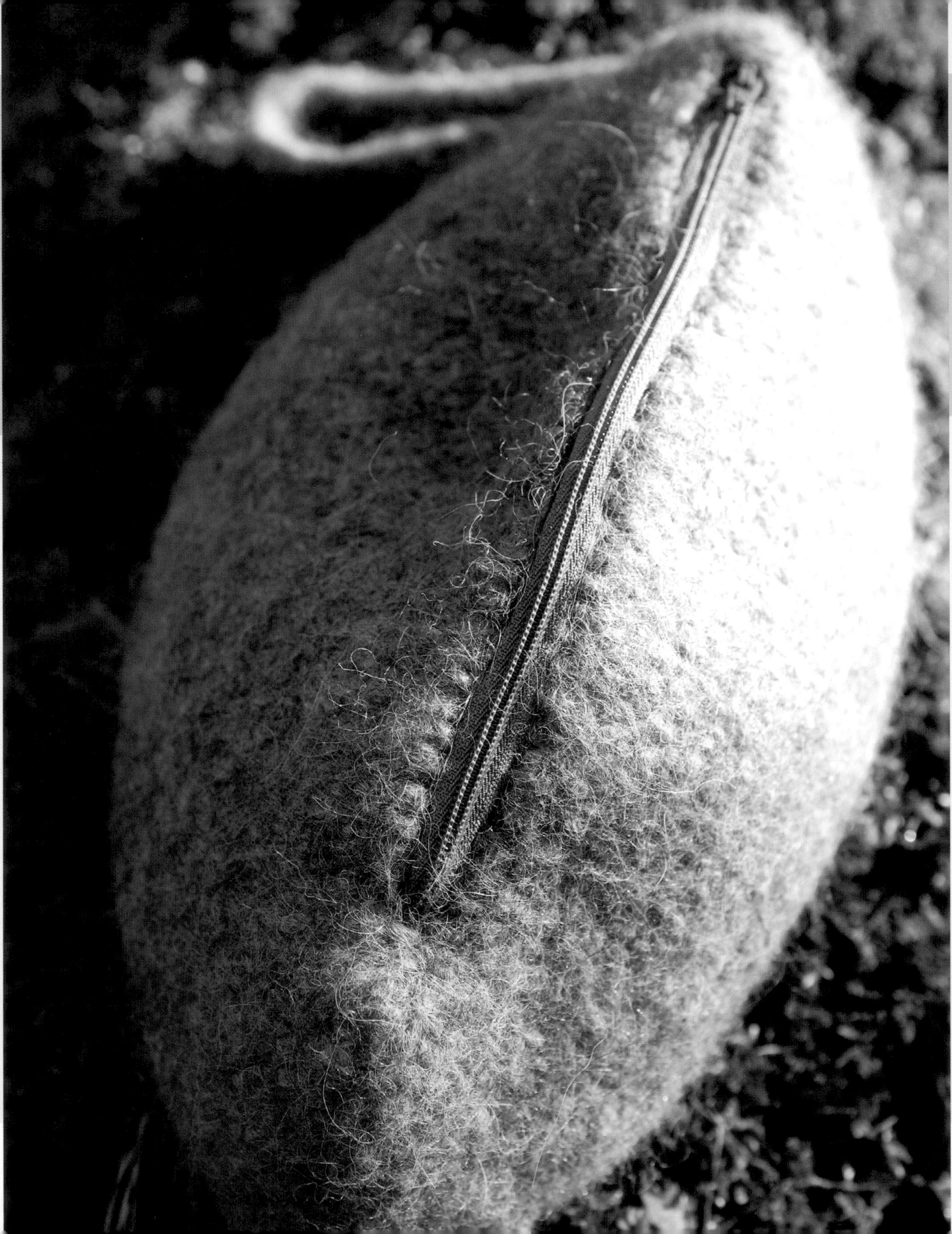

BRAZIL NUT

Why are brazil nuts so different in shape from other kernels? Did you know that within the large, round, woody fruits on the tree, individual seeds (nuts) are packed like segments of an orange? The fruits can weigh up to 5½lb (2.5kg) and contain up to 25 nuts. This large brazil nut is ideal for carrying all your bits and bobs.

COLOURS INCORPORATED

MATERIALS

❖ 150–200g aran-weight pure wool

❖ A pair of 5.5mm straight needles (US9:UK5)

❖ A pair of 4.5mm double-pointed needles (US7:UK7)

❖ 3 safety pins to indicate the right side of your work

❖ Contrast yarn to mark rows

❖ Wool needle to sew bag pieces together and finish off ends of yarn

❖ 8in (20cm) zip

❖ Matching sewing thread and needle

Note: our main bag was made with Cascade's Pastaza shade 077.
The variation was made with Garthenor's organic Hebridean wool.

DIMENSIONS

BEFORE FELTING
Ⓦ 16¼in (41.5cm) Max Ⓓ 7½in (19cm)
Max Ⓗ 7½in (19cm)

❖

AFTER FELTING
Ⓦ 11½in (29cm) Max Ⓓ 5¾in (14.5cm)
Max Ⓗ 5¾in (14.5cm)

DIFFICULTY RATING ✪ ✪

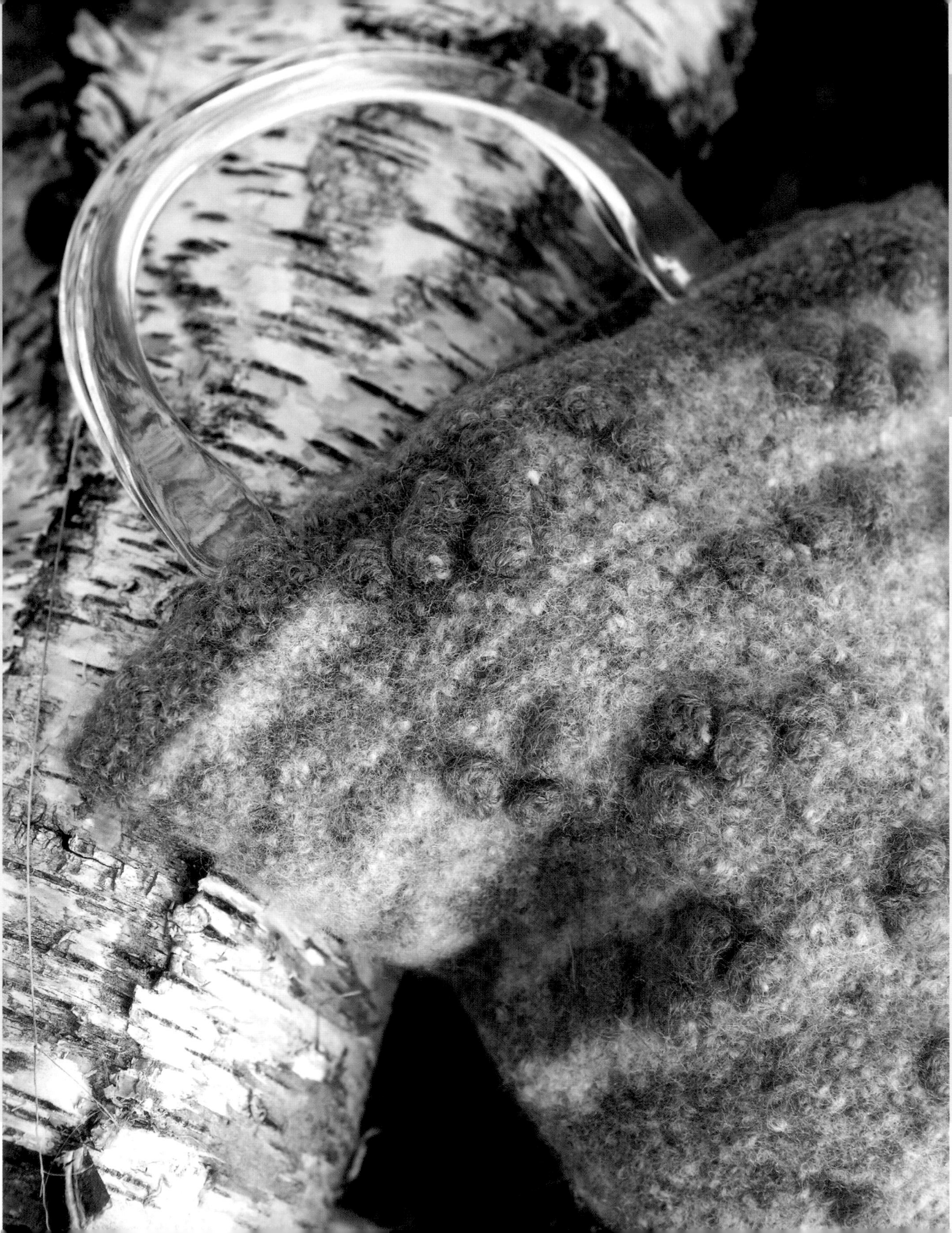

STANAGE EDGE

One of our favourite local walks is along Stanage Edge, a four-mile gritstone edge loved by rock climbers. It was also a location for a recent film version of Jane Austen's *Pride and Prejudice*. The grey of the gritstone rocks contrasts with clumps of purple and pink heather that look really beautiful in the summer and are mimicked in this design.

COLOURS INCORPORATED

MATERIALS

❖ *100g DK-weight pure wool in main colour (M)*

❖ *100g DK-weight pure wool in contrast colour (C)*

❖ *A pair of 4.5mm straight needles (US7:UK7)*

❖ *Contrast yarn to mark rows*

❖ *Wool needle to sew together and finish off ends of yarn*

❖ *A pair of bag handles, base width approximately 6in (15cm)*

Note: our example was made using Twilley's Freedom Spirit in Calm (509) and Wensleydale Longwool in Heather (19). The gentle wave at the top relies on the difference in felting characteristics of the two yarns. Substitute yarns may produce a slightly different result. Our example uses Prym's 'Viola' handles.

DIMENSIONS

BEFORE FELTING

Max **W** 13in (33cm) Max **D** 4in (10cm)
H from contrast base 16¼in (41.5cm)

❖

AFTER FELTING

Max **W** 9in (23cm) Max **D** 3in (8cm)
H from contrast base 8¾in (22.5cm)

DIFFICULTY RATING ⊕ ⊕

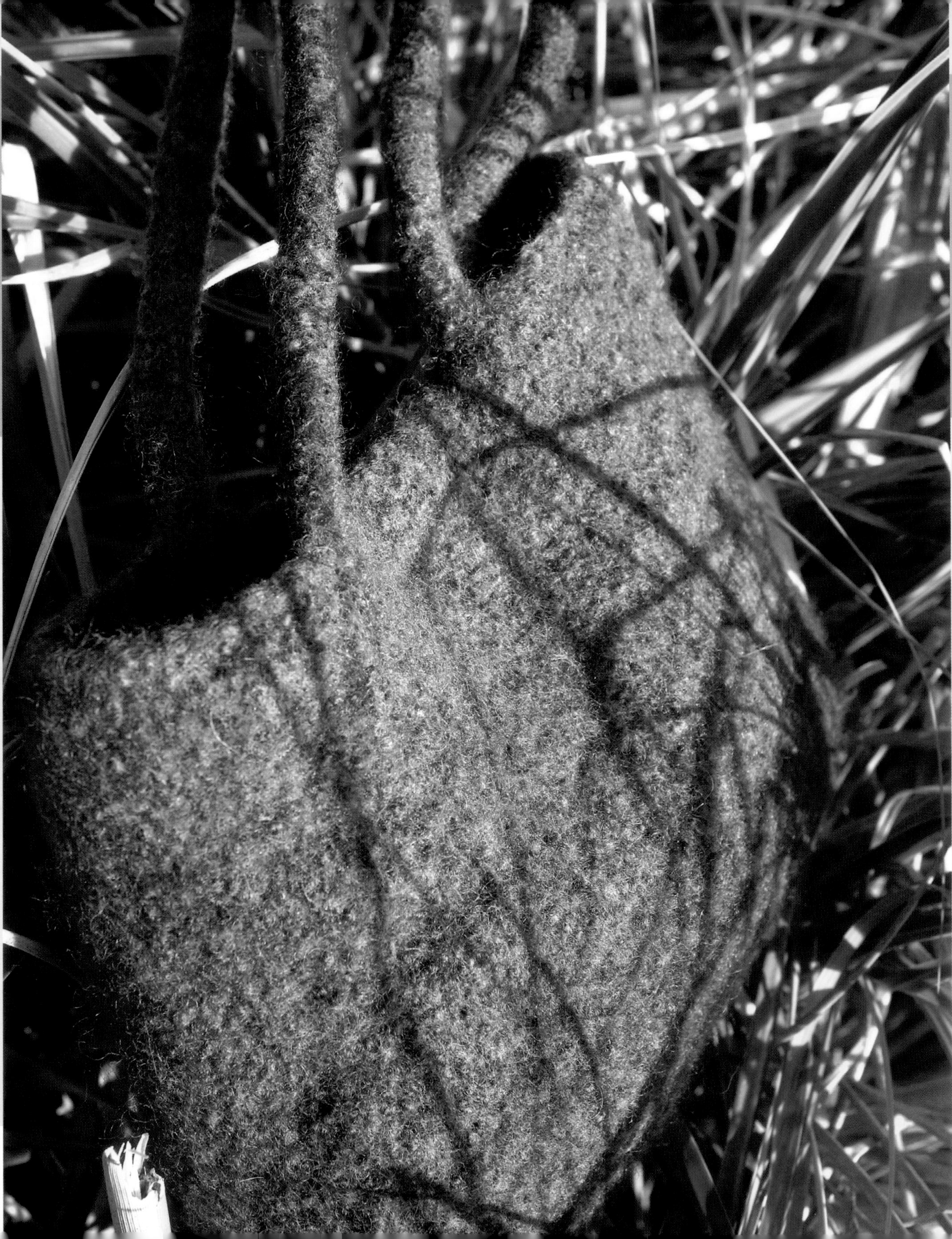

ASIAN HAT

Travelling around East and Southeast Asia you may see farmers in the fields wearing a simple straw hat as protection from sun and rain. Some are a conical shape and others have a rounded crown. The hats may be held on the head with a chin strap. You could try wearing this bag on your head, but we are confident that you will prefer to fill it with goodies instead!

COLOURS INCORPORATED

MATERIALS

❖ 300g chunky-weight pure wool

❖ A pair of 8mm straight needles (US11:UK0)

❖ An 8mm circular needle (US11: UK0)

❖ A pair of 6.5mm double-pointed needles (US10.5:UK3)

❖ 4 stitch markers

❖ 3 stitch holders or safety pins

❖ Wool needle to graft handles to bag and finish off ends of yarn

❖ Magnetic clasp (optional)

Note: our example was made using Crystal Palace Kaya, shade Ultra Blues, 0106.

DIMENSIONS

BEFORE FELTING

Base **W** 16in (41cm) Base **D** 5½in (14cm)

Bag **H** 17in (43cm)

AFTER FELTING

Base **W** 10in (25cm) Base **D** 4in (10.5cm)

Bag **H** 8½in (22cm)

DIFFICULTY RATING ⊞ ⊞

SPECIAL TECHNIQUES

Garter stitch *see page 145*
Stocking stitch *see page 145*
Using stitch markers *see page 147*

Working in the round *see pages 148–9*
Making an I-cord *see page 150*
Grafting stitches *see page 151*

Felting *see page 152*
Attaching a magnetic clasp *see page 155*

INSTRUCTIONS

This bag is worked using a circular needle.

The base

Using the 8mm straight needles cast on 42 sts and knit 30 rows to form a garter-stitch base. Change to the circular needle and knit across the sts from the straight needle.

Pick up and knit 20 sts along the short edge of the base, 42 sts along the second long edge and 20 sts along the second short edge, placing a stitch marker at each corner (124 sts).

Knit 15 rounds, moving the markers across as they are reached.

Round 16: Decrease by 1 st before and after each corner marker by knitting 2 sts together (116 sts). Decrease in the same way on rows 31 (108 sts), 46 (100 sts) and 61 (92 sts).

The upper edge

Purl 1 round, knit 1 round, purl 1 round.

Next round: From the start of round marker, knit 11 sts. Cast off 12 sts. *K4 and place the 5 sts on your needle on a stitch holder or safety pin**. Cast off 24 sts. Work * to ** once. Cast off 12 sts. Work * to ** once. Cast off 24 sts. Knit to end (5 sts remain on needle). *Note: there should now be a total of four sets of 5 sts to form the handles.*

Transfer the set of 5 sts from the needle to a double-pointed needle and work in I-cord for 39in (100cm). Graft these stitches to the remaining 5 sts on the same long side of the bag. Rejoin yarn and repeat for the handle on the other side, to match.

Finish off all ends of yarn by weaving into the work before felting.

FELTING

Felt the bag in the washing machine. Our example felted sufficiently with one 140°F (60°C) wash.

Attaching a clasp

If you wish, fasten a magnetic clasp to either side of the upper edge of your bag, on the inside.

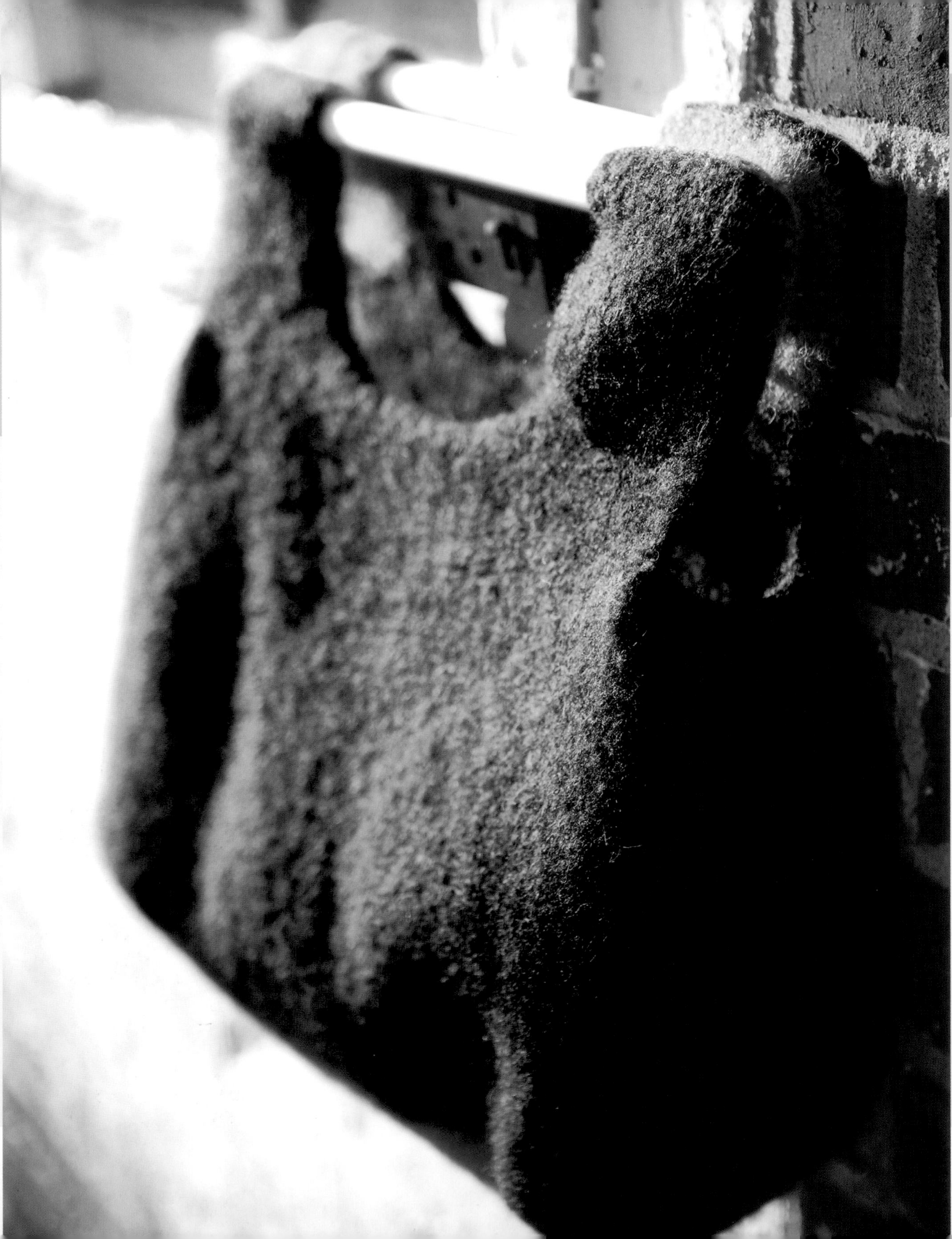

PROJECT BAG

Purple and turquoise were really popular colours back in the 1970s and, as so often happens, fashion has turned full circle and they are bang up to date again. This bag is ideal for carrying your latest knitting project around. It can, of course be knitted in your own favourite shades. Stain or paint the wooden handles to further enhance the bag.

COLOURS INCORPORATED

MATERIALS

❖ *400g chunky-weight pure wool in main colour (M)*

❖ *100g chunky-weight pure wool in contrast colour (C)*

❖ *A pair of 8mm straight needles (US11:UK0)*

❖ *Small amount of contrast yarn to mark seams*

❖ *Stitch holder*

❖ *Wool needle to sew seams and finish off ends of yarn*

❖ *2 lengths of 18mm dowel, approximately 12½in (32cm)*

Note: our example was made using Texere chunky wool in Purple (M), and Turquoise (C).

DIMENSIONS

BEFORE FELTING

W 16¼in (41cm) Base **D** 7in (18cm)

H 17in (43cm) (2¼in [59cm] to top of handle)

❖

AFTER FELTING

W 12½in (32cm) **D** 6¼in (16cm)

H 11in (28cm) (15¾in [40cm] to top of handle)

DIFFICULTY RATING ⊕ ⊕

SPECIAL TECHNIQUES
Garter stitch *see page 145*
Stocking stitch *see page 145*

Using stitch markers *see page 147*

Felting *see page 152*

INSTRUCTIONS

This bag is made by knitting the base, then knitting up each side individually and sewing seams together before felting. The wooden handle is inserted after felting.

The base

Using the 8mm straight needles and C, cast on 46 sts and knit 40 rows in garter stitch. Without casting off, change to M to work the sides in stocking stitch with garter-stitch edges.

The first side

Row 1: Knit.
Row 2: K3, purl to last 3 sts, k3.

Repeat the last 2 rows until a total of 64 rows have been worked in M. Mark both sides of the last row worked to help to position the side panels when sewing together.

The upper edge

Next row: Knit.
Next row: K3, p6, k28, p6, k3.
Repeat the last 2 rows once more, making a total of 4 rows in this pattern.

Shaping the straps

Straps are in stocking stitch, with a 3-sts garter-stitch edge border and panel round the middle opening.

Next row: Knit 18 sts, cast off 10 sts, knit to end of row, turn.
Next row: *k3, p6, knit to end of row**.
Place the remaining set of 18 sts on a stitch holder.

Next row: K2tog, knit to end of row.
Next row: Work * to ** as above.

Continue to shape at the inside edge of the strap by repeating the last 2 rows, until 12 sts remain, ending with a WS row. Work 11 rows in stocking-stitch pattern with garter-stitch side edges, without further shaping.

Next row (WS facing): Knit to produce a garter-stitch ridge that indicates the position of the fold. Join in C and, beginning with a knit row, work a further 20 rows in stocking-stitch pattern with garter stitch side edges.
Cast off all stitches.

WS facing, rejoin the yarn to those on the stitch holder and work a second handle, reversing shaping by decreasing at the end of RS rows.

The second side

With RS facing and using M, pick up and knit 46 sts from the second long side of the base. Starting with the second row of the pattern, complete to match the first side.

Side panels

With RS facing and using M, pick up and knit 28 sts from one of the short sides of the base. Starting with the second row of the stocking-stitch pattern with garter-stitch side edges, work 59 rows. At this point, the side will measure approximately 15–16in (38–40cm) from the base. Knit 4 rows. Cast off all stitches. Repeat on the second short side of the base.

Making up

Sew the side panels to the front and back, matching the top edge of the two side panels with the contrast yarn markers on the edges of the front and back. To encourage the side panel to pleat inwards, sew the top of the garter-stitch borders of the side panels to those on the front and back of your bag.

Fold the handle strap at the garter-stitch ridge towards the inside of the bag, and sew the outer and lower edges in place. The inside edge is left open until after felting.

Finish off all ends of yarn by weaving into the work before felting.

FELTING

Felt the bag in the washing machine. Our example felted sufficiently with one 140°F (60°C) wash. When dry, fold each of the side panels in half, inwards, at the top. Sew the fold together neatly, at the top, for approximately ½in (1.5cm). This will encourage the side panels to fold inwards when the bag is only partly full.

Attaching the handle

Cut the dowel to size if necessary: when inserted in the handles, it should reach fully from one side edge to the other. Insert each end of the dowel into the two folded straps on the front of the bag. Sew the inside seam securely. Repeat on the other side of the bag.

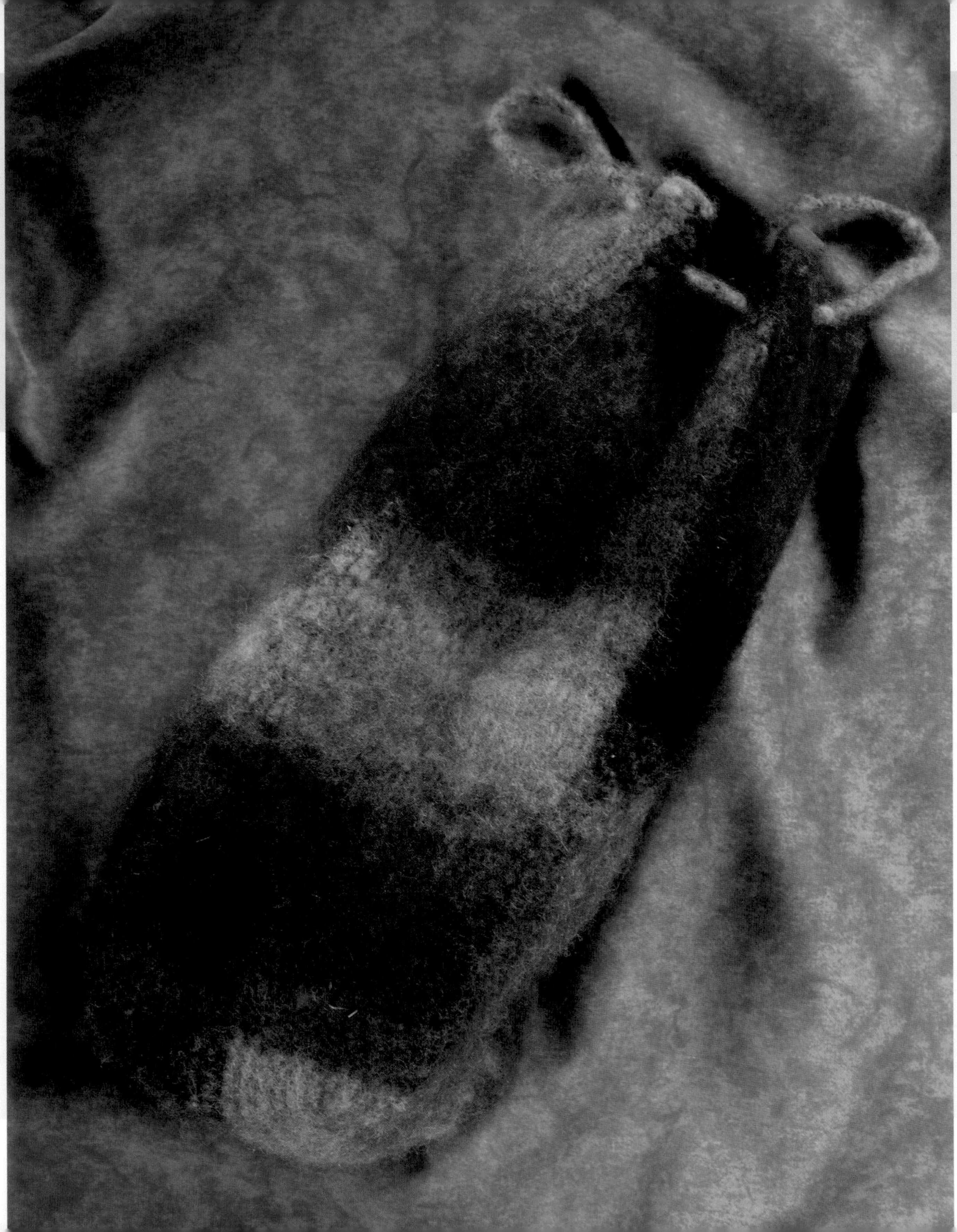

GIFT BAG

It's always a treat to receive an unusually wrapped present, and this bag certainly fits the bill: it's ideal for making a small gift look really special. It can be made in a tall version that is suitable for a bottle of wine, or a short version that is ideal for a small item such as a plant or a box of chocolates.

COLOURS INCORPORATED

MATERIALS

❖ *150g (100g) aran-weight pure wool*

❖ *A pair of 5.5mm straight needles (US9:UK5)*

❖ *Wool needle to sew bag pieces together and finish off ends of yarn*

Note: our main bag is made with Noro Kureyon, shade number 170 and the variation with Debbie Bliss Donegal Luxury Tweed in orange, shade number 360013.

DIMENSIONS

BEFORE FELTING

Ⓦ 5¾in (14.5cm) Ⓓ 5¾in (14.5cm)

Ⓗ 16½in (variation: 9in) (42[23]cm)

❖

AFTER FELTING

Ⓦ 4¾in (12cm) Ⓓ 4¾in (12cm)

Ⓗ 11½in (variation: 5½in) (29[14]cm)

DIFFICULTY RATING ⊕

INSTRUCTIONS

The larger version is given first, with the smaller version in brackets.

The base

Using the 5.5mm straight needles, cast on 23 sts and knit 42 rows in garter stitch.

The first side

Starting with a knit row, work 88 (44) rows in stocking stitch. At this stage, the bag will measure approximately 15¾in (40cm) or 7½in (19cm).

Next row (eyelet): K2, cast off 2 sts, knit to last 4 sts, cast off 2 sts, knit to end.
Next row: Purl all stitches casting on 2 sts over each cast-off section.

Knit 4 rows to give a garter-stitch upper edge, then cast off all stitches k-wise.

The second side

With RS facing, pick up and knit 23 sts from the next side edge of the base. Starting with a purl row, work 87 (43) rows in stocking stitch. Work the eyelet rows and the garter-stitch band as on the first side, then cast off all stitches k-wise.

Third and fourth sides

Repeat the instructions for the second side to make the remaining two sides.

Note: you will now have a garter-stitch base with the four sides making a cross shape. The base will be approximately square, but may not remain square after felting, due to differences in shrinkage during felting for alternative wools.

Making up

Sew the four sides together to create an upright cuboid-shaped bag.

Finish off all ends of yarn by weaving into the work before felting.

The handle

Cut three lengths of yarn, each 71in (180cm) long and, holding the three ends together, fold the bundle in half. Loosely knot the fold. There will now be six loose lengths of yarn joined together at the fold at the top. Divide the lengths of yarn into three pairs and plait these together along the full length. Knot the end.

Thread the plaited handle in and out through the eyelets at the top of the bag. Knot both ends of the handle firmly together.

FELTING

Felt the bag in the washing machine. Our examples felted sufficiently with two 140°F (60°C) washes.

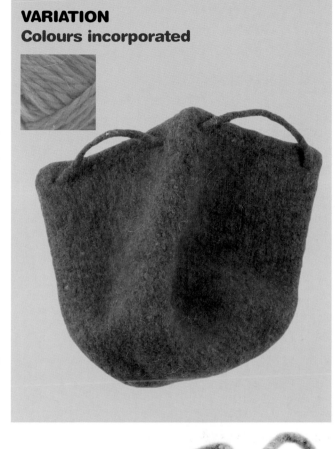

VARIATION
Colours incorporated

133

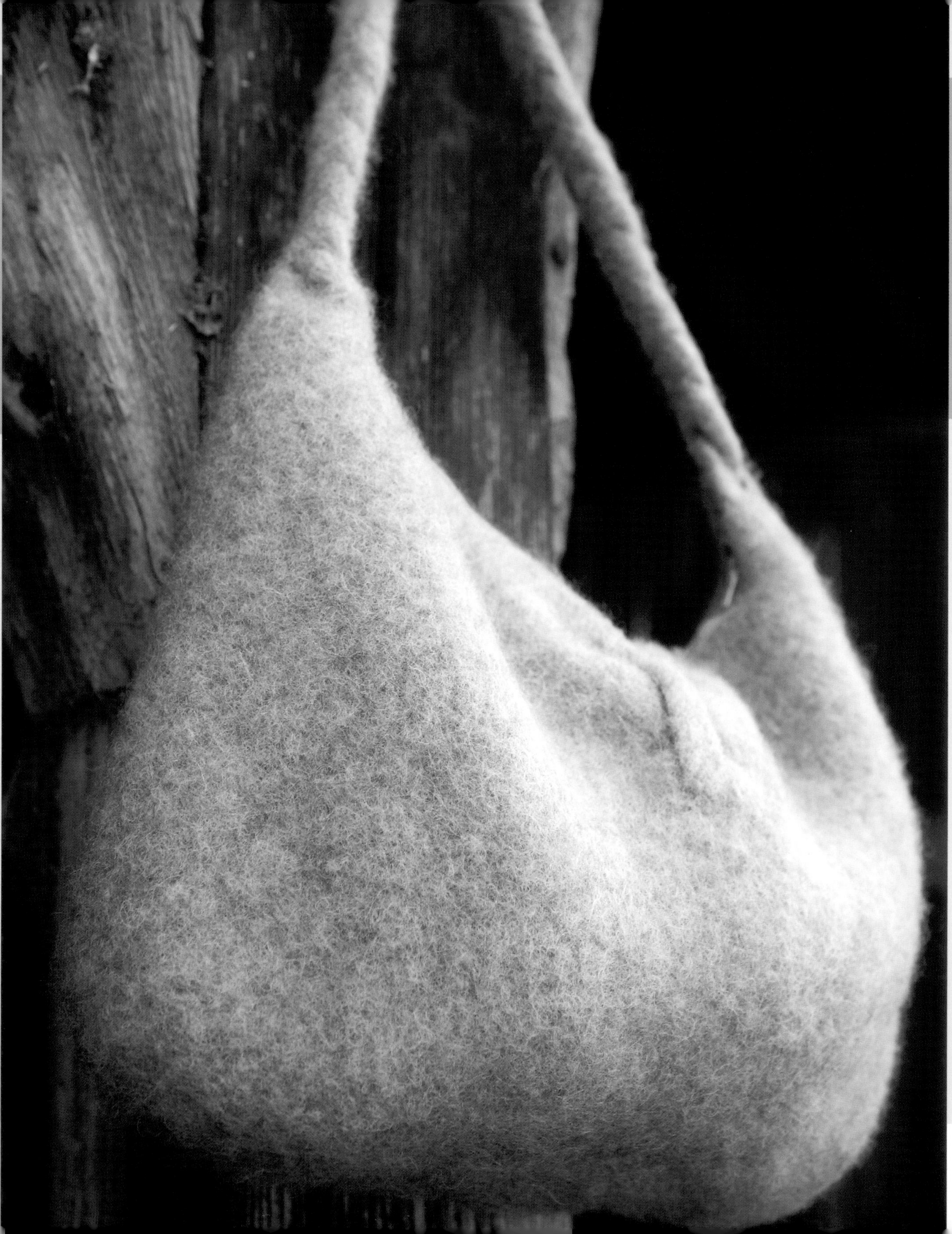

RETRO STYLE

The introduction of the 'talkies' in the 1930s produced a host of glamorous and sensuous film stars, and fashion began to celebrate natural womanly curves. This was the time of big bands, dancing and endless nightlife. Inspired by those times, this bag makes use of a zip, the decorative yet functional closure promoted by leading Paris fashion designer Elsa Schiaparelli in 1933.

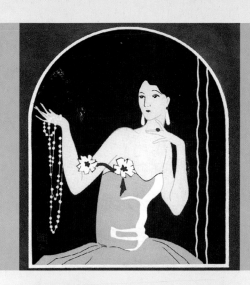

COLOURS INCORPORATED

MATERIALS

❖ *200g DK-weight pure wool*

❖ *A pair of 4.5mm straight needles (US7:UK7)*

❖ *A 4.5mm circular needle (US7:UK7)*

❖ *A pair of 4.5mm double-pointed needles (US7:UK7)*

❖ *4 stitch markers made from contrast yarn*

❖ *3 safety pins or stitch holders*

❖ *Wool needle to join bag and finish off ends of yarn*

❖ *12in (30cm) zip with sewing needle and matching thread (optional)*

Note: our examples were made using Sheepfold's Heather range in DK. The main bag is in Forget-me-knot and the variation is in Indigo.

DIMENSIONS

BEFORE FELTING

W 15in (38cm) **D** 4¼in (11cm)

H at centre 11½in (29cm)

❖

AFTER FELTING

W 11in (28cm) **D** 3½in (9cm)

H at centre 8in (20.5cm)

DIFFICULTY RATING ✪ ✪ ✪

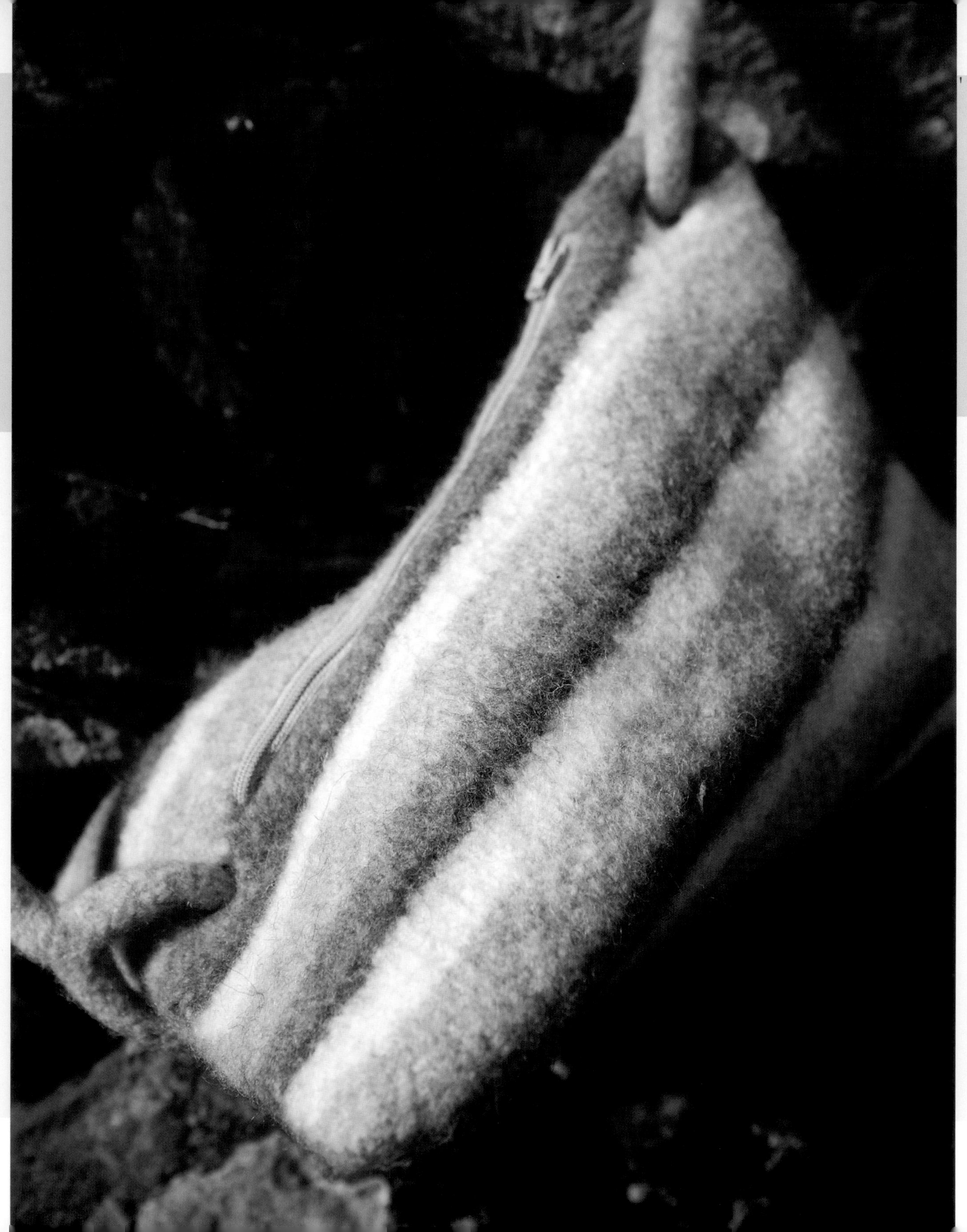

HUMBUG

Ebenezer Scrooge apart, the word 'humbug' has very happy associations with the traditional, stripy hard-boiled peppermint sweets. The shape varies: it can be round, oblong or rather like a three-sided pyramid, formed when the confectioner twists the rolled strips of confectionery between cuts. A similar shape to the latter makes this a fun bag with a difference.

COLOURS INCORPORATED

MATERIALS

❖ *100g DK-weight pure wool in main colour (M)*

❖ *50g DK-weight pure wool in each of 3 contrast colours (C1, C2 and C3))*

❖ *A pair of 4.5mm straight needles (US7:UK7)*

❖ *A pair of 4.5mm double-pointed needles (US7:UK7)*

❖ *Contrast yarn to mark rows*

❖ *Wool needle to join bag and finish off ends of yarn*

❖ *8in (20cm) zip*

❖ *Sewing needle and matching thread*

Note: examples here use Sirdar Eco Wool. The main bag uses Natural 201 (M), Ecru 200 (C1), Earth 203 (C2) and Clay 202 (C3), the variation the same colours in a different order: Earth (M), Natural (C1), Clay (C2) and Ecru (C3).

DIMENSIONS

BEFORE FELTING

Ⓦ 13½in (34cm) Ⓓ 11in (28cm)

Ⓗ 11in (28cm)

❖

AFTER FELTING

Ⓦ 10½in (26.5cm) Ⓓ 7¼in (19cm)

Ⓗ 7½in (19cm)

DIFFICULTY RATING ⊕

TECHNIQUES

CHOOSING YARN

Felting takes place when the microscopic scales on the animal hairs lock together. This requires a combination of water, movement and heat, which can be achieved in a washing machine. The ease with which this happens varies not only between animals but also between breeds of sheep. Fibres from camelids (llama and alpaca) felt very easily while fleece from some breeds of sheep, such as Ryeland, hardly felts at all. All the wools used in this book have been thoroughly tested, but measurements must be regarded only as an indication. The exact size of the finished bag will depend on both the yarn selected and the temperature in your machine.

Superwash or machine-washable yarn has been treated to remove its scales, so will not felt even if boiled. Synthetic yarns, such as acrylic or polyester, do not have scales, so cannot be felted. This can be used to good effect when inserting a contrast section in your bag (see Icy Grass, page 8).

Note: if using a substitute yarn we strongly recommend that you test it (see page 152) before knitting a project.

TENSION

When following a pattern for a garment, tension is very important in order to achieve a good fit. When work is felted, particularly when making a bag, this does not apply. In fact, tension should be kept loose to allow space for the work to shrink during the felting process. This is typically achieved by working with needles one or more sizes larger than stated on the ball band.

If the tension is too tight the felting process may be limited and the stitches will remain visible. Personal preference and the felting process used will decide how much stitch definition is lost. We prefer to lose the visibility of the stitches, so the bags appear to be made by magic!

Casting on

CASTING ON

The basic cast on produces a purl stitch as a base.

1 Make a slip knot and place on the left-hand needle. Insert the right-hand needle into the loop and wrap the yarn round the needles as shown.

2 Using the point of the right-hand needle, pull the yarn through the first loop to create a second loop.

3 Slide it onto the left-hand needle so there are two loops on the needle.

Repeat step 2 and 3 until you have the desired number of stitches on your needle.

CASTING OFF

1 Knit two stitches using the right-hand needle, then slip the first stitch over the second and let it drop over the needle as shown.

2 Knit another stitch so there are two stitches on the right-hand needle. Repeat the process. When only one stitch remains, break yarn and thread through the stitch.

Casting off

Knit stitch

KNIT STITCH

1 Hold the needle with the cast-on stitches in your left hand. Place the tip of the empty right-hand needle into the first stitch. Wrap the yarn around as for casting on.

2 Pull the yarn through the needle to create a new loop.

3 Slip the new stitch on to the right-hand needle.

Continue in the same way for each stitch on the left-hand needle.

To start a new row, exchange the needles so that the left needle is full once again and repeat these instructions.

PURL STITCH

1 Hold the yarn to the front of the work as shown.

2 Place the right needle into the first stitch from back to front. Wrap the yarn around the right needle in an anti-clockwise direction as shown.

3 Bring the needle down and back through the stitch, and pull through.

Purl stitch

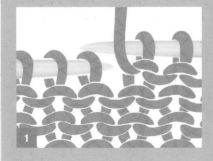
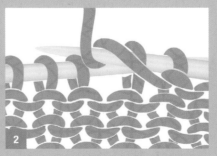

TYPES OF STITCH

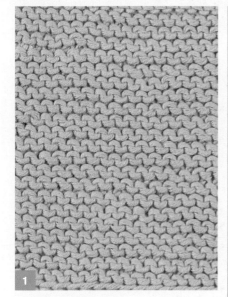

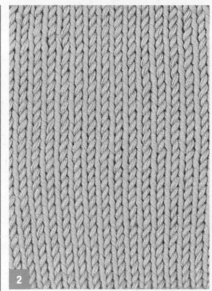

1 GARTER STITCH

For a flat piece: knit every row.
When knitting in the round: knit 1
round, purl 1 round.

2 STOCKING STITCH

For a flat piece: knit RS rows; purl
WS rows.
When knitting in the round: knit
every round.

3 MOSS STITCH

Starting with an even number
of stitches:
Row 1: (K1, P1) to end.
Row 2: (P1, K1) to end.
Rep rows 1 and 2 to form pattern.
Starting with an odd number of
stitches:
Row 1: *K1, P1, rep from * to last
st, K1.
Rep to form pattern.

INTARSIA

When combining two or more yarns in a design that will be felted it is important to use the intarsia technique. In this, separate balls of yarn are used to avoid the need to carry or weave lengths across the back of the work.

First wind several small bobbins of each colour, either as a centre-pull butterfly or onto plastic or card bobbins. Do not wind too much yarn or the bobbins will be too large and heavy. It is essential that all wools in your design should felt to the same degree so test samples first, or select wool of the same type or from the same breed of sheep.

Begin with the first row of the chart, starting at the lower right-hand corner and working right to left. Each square in the grid represents a single stitch, knitted on the right side and purled on the wrong side. Work the second and alternate rows from left to right. When changing colour, drop the first yarn and bring up the second, crossing or twisting the yarns over each other on every row to link the two colour blocks and prevent holes in the work.

The loops of yarn formed at the back of the piece must be loose, or the edges of the colour blocks will become crumpled and uneven when felted. Take care that the bobbins at the back of your work do not become tangled.

This technique is best for flat knitting rather than knitting in the round, as each coloured yarn ends up in approximately the correct place for the next row. Kilim Shopper (see page 38) and Skerry (see page 48) are knitted this way. An exception is when a pattern repeats rapidly, such as Inca Hat (see page 28).

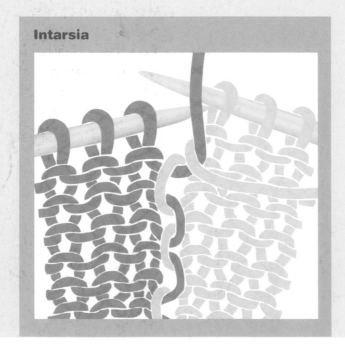

Intarsia

Picking up stitches

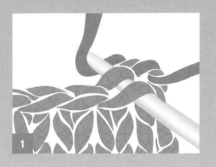

PICKING UP STITCHES

1 Hold the work with your left thumb and forefinger. Take a needle in your right hand and insert the point through the loops at the edge of the work.

2 Wrap the yarn round the needle as if to knit the stitch and then draw through to form a stitch on the needle.

3 Continue to pick up loops evenly along the edge of the work until the required number of stitches has been picked up.

USING STITCH MARKERS

Marking certain points in your work makes it far easier to count stitches and place handles. Plastic or beaded loops may be used, but we prefer to use contrasting waste yarn.

1 Make a simple overhand knot in a short length of waste yarn.

2 It is best to mark the beginning/ end of a round in a different colour to the corner markers to show where the round starts.

3 The loops are slipped across when working, so moving up the work with each row. In some patterns a stitch is

'permanently' marked; for example, to show where to pick up stitches for a handle. To do this, thread a piece of waste yarn through the stitch and knot loosely. These markers remain attached to the marked stitch until the finishing stage. Remove all markers before felting the bag.

Using stitch markers

WORKING IN THE ROUND

Where a design is worked 'in the round' we recommend using a circular needle. Double-pointed needles may be used if you prefer.

Using a circular needle

Cast on as usual, or pick up stitches as advised in your instructions, using the ends of the circular needle in the same way as a pair of needles. We recommend that you place a stitch marker on your needle to denote the beginning/end of the round. Some patterns will also advise the use of additional stitch markers to mark the corners of the bag.

1 Making sure the cast on row is not twisted, close the loop by bringing the ends of the cast-on row together and knitting around the circle.

In most patterns the rounds will be knitted, giving the appearance of stocking stitch. Some patterns may tell you to purl certain rows; for example, at the top of the bag to stop the edge curling when felted.

For most designs a 31½in (80cm) circular needle is used. If this is a little too long near the base of the bag, pull a loop of the flexible cord out until there is enough stretch in the work to fill the remaining length of the needle. Alternatively, change to a shorter circular needle.

2 Continue working without turning, slipping each stitch marker across as you reach it.

Using a circular needle

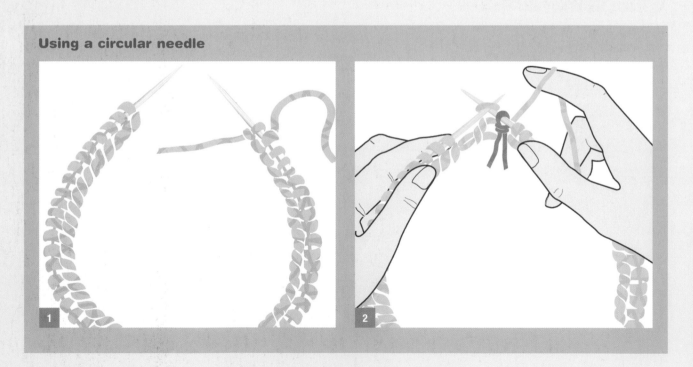

Using double-pointed needles

Knitting in the round usually requires 4 or 5 needles, but more can be used if preferred.

1 Cast on the required number of stitches, beginning with two needles and introducing additional needles as needed. Keep one needle aside to use as the 'working' needle. When casting on a small number of stitches it may be easier do this on just one needle, then slip them evenly across the other needles.

2 Place stitch markers to denote the beginning and end of the round. Taking care not to twist the cast on row, work the stitches from each needle in turn to close the circle. Without turning, continue working the stitches, slipping the stitch marker across as it is reached.

As with a circular needle, if all stitches are knitted the work will appear as stocking stitch.

Using double-pointed needles

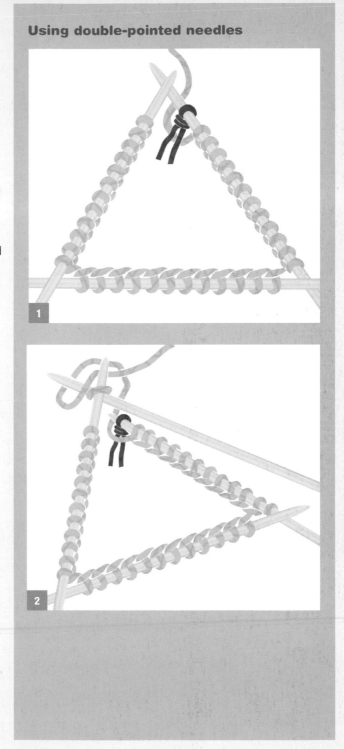

MAKING AN I-CORD

Using double-pointed needles, cast on the required number of sts – typically 5 sts. **Do not turn work**. Slide sts to the opposite end of the needle, then take the yarn firmly across the back of work. Knit sts again. Repeat to desired length. Cast off, or follow instructions in pattern. An I-cord is often grafted to stitches left on a holder after working another part of the pattern.

MAKING AN ATTACHED I-CORD

Using double-pointed needles, cast on the required number of stitches – typically 4 sts – then pick up and knit 1 st along the edge of your knitted piece. **Do not turn work**. Slide the stitches to the opposite end of the needle, take the yarn firmly across the back of work. Knit across until 2sts remain, k2tog through the back of the loops then pick up and knit 1 st from the edge of your knitted piece. Repeat until you have an attached I-cord in the required position, typically around the bag or along the upper edge. Cast off all stitches.

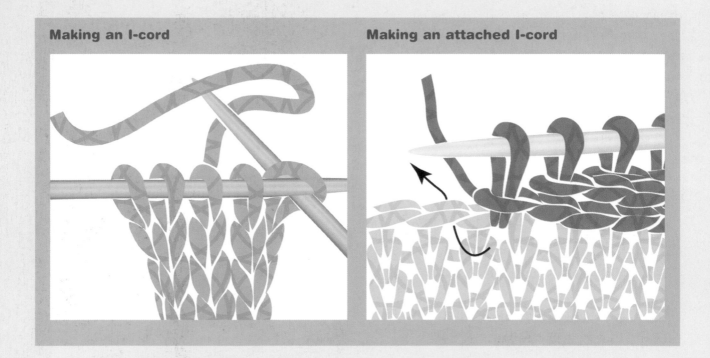

Making an I-cord

Making an attached I-cord

JOINING PIECES

Sewing seams

The side or base seams of bags not knitted in the round will need to be joined using a simple slipstitch technique. Take care not to pull the stitches too tight.

Grafting stitches

This method of invisible joining, known as Kitchener stitch, is used in our patterns to join handles or loops.

1 Pick up the required number of loops or divide the reserved stitches evenly between a pair of needles. Thread the working yarn on to a wool needle. Holding the needles parallel, pass the wool needle, as if to knit, through the first stitch of the front needle.

2 Pass the wool needle, as if to purl, through the second stitch on the front needle while allowing the first stitch to slip off.

3 Pass the wool needle, as if to purl, through the first stitch on the back needle.

4 Then, as if to knit, pass the wool needle through the second stitch on the back needle while allowing the first stitch to slip off.

Repeat this cycle until all the stitches are used up. Fasten off the working yarn securely.

Kitchener stitch

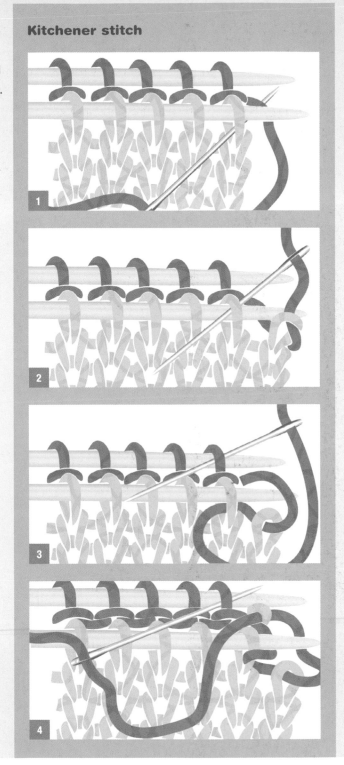

FELTING

If using a yarn you have not felted before, knit a few swatches and test them at different temperatures and different wash cycles. The degree of felting will depend on temperature, soap use, agitation, time and wool selected. Yarns containing fibres from camelids, such as those containing llama or alpaca, may only need a single wash at 86°F (30°C), while wool from some breeds of sheep may require temperatures as high as 194°F (90°C).

The degree of felting is a personal choice. Most of the bags in this book are felted until the stitches are no longer visible, and the temperature and number of cycles to achieve this effect are given. If you prefer to felt to a lesser degree, the resulting bags will be slightly larger than indicated. As a guide, most knitted pieces should reduce to approximately one-half to two-thirds their original size and height will often reduce more than width. Remember that machine-washable and superwash wools, or synthetic fibres, such as polyester or acrylic, will not felt however high the temperature or long the cycle.

To felt using a washing machine, put the item in a zippered mesh bag or pillowcase. Place in the machine along with a couple of towels or pairs of jeans to give the necessary agitation. You may also use dolly washer balls that are designed to increase action in the washing machine. Add a small amount of washing powder or liquid wash (around 1tsp/5ml) but no fabric conditioner. Remember to check your bag between wash cycles.

For front loaders, select short washes and low-level spin options if available, as these will reduce the risk of crumpling the bag. For top-loaders, set to a hot wash with a low water level and maximum agitation. With these washers felting may be checked every five to ten minutes, but take care when removing the bag from the hot water and use tongs if possible. If there has been no rinse cycle, rinse by hand using warm water once felted.

It is important to check your bag regularly between or during wash cycles to monitor the level of felting. This is particularly important for flat bag shapes, as the front and back sometimes become loosely felted together and you may need to separate them. You can be quite firm doing this; the bag will not suffer.

When felted to the desired level, remove the bag from the machine, smooth out any crumples or creases, and leave somewhere warm to dry out completely. If the bag is a rounded rather than a flat shape, place a plastic bag filled with crumpled newspaper inside to form the appropriate shape before leaving to dry. Drying may take up to two to three days, depending on temperature, so be patient.

If using a yarn spun with mixed-length fibres, such as some of the specific sheep breeds or camelids, wipe out the inside of your machine to remove all the loose fibres once felting is complete.

Swatches

Below are the results produced from the swatches
indicated, which were knitted with wool and baby llama.

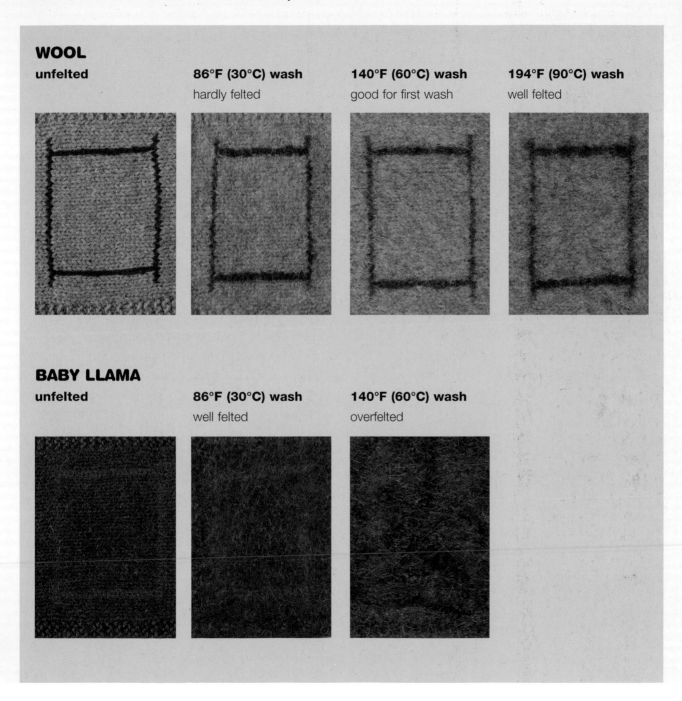

WOOL

unfelted	86°F (30°C) wash	140°F (60°C) wash	194°F (90°C) wash
	hardly felted	good for first wash	well felted

BABY LLAMA

unfelted	86°F (30°C) wash	140°F (60°C) wash
	well felted	overfelted

ATTACHING A ZIP

A zip size has been given where appropriate, but it is best to check the exact size required when the bag is felted. If the zip is a little too short, close up any gap either end using the knitting yarn. If it is too long, simply leave the excess length inside the bag and sew in place with matching thread.

1 To insert the zip, pin one side to one edge in the opening of the felted bag. The edge should be approximately ⅛ in (3–4mm) from the teeth of the zip. It may help to fold the fabric edging of the zip underneath so it does not get caught when opening and closing your zip later. With small stitches, sew the zip in place using sewing thread. The stitches should bed into the felt so will not be easily visible.

2 Open the zip, pin the second side to the second side of the opening and sew the two pieces together, as before. To neaten the inside, slipstitch the fabric edge of the zip to the felted bag, again using small stitches, and making sure they are not visible on the outside.

Attaching a zip

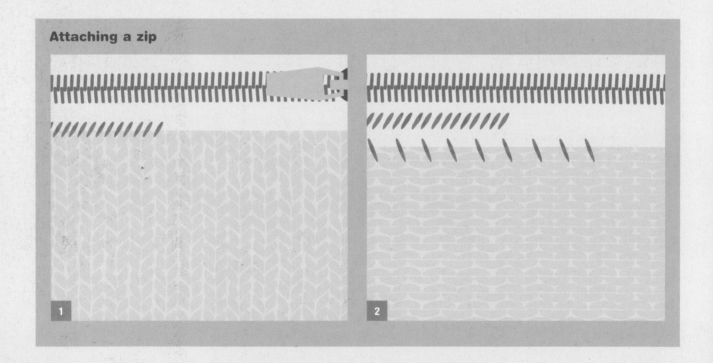

ATTACHING A MAGNETIC CLASP

It is best to attach the clasp to some crossgrain ribbon, strengthened with iron-on interfacing if necessary. The ribbon can then be sewn to the inside of your bag so the back of the clasp is 'invisible'.

1 Using a pencil, mark the position for the prongs of the clasp on the ribbon, using the backing plate as a guide.

2 Cut small slits in the ribbon where marked. Pass the prongs of the clasp through to the wrong (interfaced) side.

3 Place the backing plate over the pair of prongs and fold them over firmly towards the centre. If necessary, place the clasp on a block of wood or thick card and use a small hammer to assist in folding the prongs over.

4 Fold the raw edges of the ribbon to the wrong side and, using matching thread, sew the ribbon and attached clasp to the inside of the bag.

Repeat for the second part of the clasp, carefully aligning with the first part of the clasp when sewing inside the bag.

Attaching a magnetic clasp

Making tassels

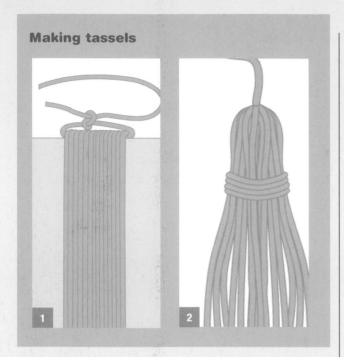

MAKING TASSELS

1 Take a piece of stiff card, approximately 3in (8cm) wide, and wrap yarn round it several times. Secure this bundle with a separate length of yarn threaded through at one end, leaving long ends, then cut the bundle at the opposite edge.

2 Keeping the bundle folded in half, wind a separate length of yarn a few times round the whole bundle, including the long ends of the tie, approximately ¾in (2cm) below the fold, to form the head of the tassel.

3 Tie the two ends of this length of yarn together tightly. Trim all the ends of yarn at the base of the tassel to give a tidy finish. If you want a more bushy tassel, unroll and separate the strands of yarn.

MAKING FRINGE TASSELS

Cut lengths of yarn and fold in half. Using a crochet hook, pull the fold through the lower edge of the bag **(1)** to make a loop **(2)**. Pass the ends of the bundle through the loop and pull firmly to neaten and secure **(3)**. Repeat along the length required. Fringing should be attached after felting.

Making fringe tassels

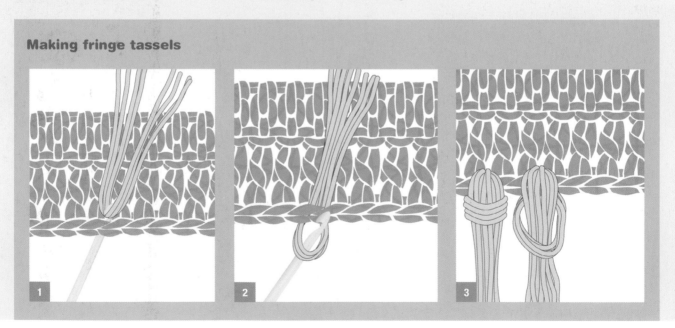

ABBREVIATIONS

C	contrast colour
cm	centimetre
DK	double knit
g	gram (weight)
in	inches
K	knit
K2tog	decrease by knitting 2 stitches together
k-wise	by knitting the stitch
M	main colour
mB	instructions given in pattern(s)
mfB	instructions given in pattern(s)
mm	millimetre
m1	instructions given in pattern(s)
P	purl
psso	pass the slipped stitch over
P2tog	purl 2 together
p-wise	by purling the stitch
RS	right side
sl	slip
st(s)	stitch(es)
tbl	through back of loop
tog	together
WS	wrong side
yon	yarn over needle
°C	degrees centrigrade
°F	degrees fahrenheit
Yf	yarn forward
*, **	work instructions between * and **, then repeat as directed

CONVERSIONS

YARN WEIGHT CONVERSIONS

UK	US
4-ply	Sport
Double knitting	Light worsted
Aran	Fisherman/Worsted
Chunky	Bulky
Super Chunky	Extra Bulky

KNITTING NEEDLE CONVERSIONS

UK	Metric	US
14	2mm	0
13	2.25mm	1
12	2.75mm	2
11	3mm	–
10	3.25mm	3
–	3.5mm	4
9	3.75mm	5
8	4mm	6
7	4.5mm	7
6	5mm	8
5	5.5mm	9
4	6mm	10
3	6.5mm	10.5
2	7mm	10.5
1	7.5mm	11
0	8mm	11
00	9mm	13
000	10mm	15

SUPPLIERS

www.colinette.com

This site includes a shop where the Colinette yarn used in this book can be purchased worldwide.

T: +44 (0)1938 810128

www.iknit.org.uk

This site includes a shop where some of the yarns in this book can be purchased worldwide. These include those from Colinette, Garthenor Organic, Jamieson's Shetland, Sirdar and Wensleydale Longwool.

T: +44 (0)20 7261 1338

E: info@iknit.org.uk

www.injabulo.com

This site includes a shop where the incomparable buttons can be purchased worldwide. Injabulo also let you know the sales events that they will be attending, where the buttons can be seen and purchased.

T: +44 (0)1832 274881

E: info@injabulo.com

www.jamiesonsshetland.co.uk

This site includes a shop where the Jamieson's Shetland yarn used in this book can be purchased. It also lists worldwide stockists.

T: +44 (0)1595 693 114

E: info@jamiesonsofshetland.co.uk

www.paviyarns.co.uk

Some of the yarns used in this book can be purchased from this online shop worldwide. These include those from Cascade, Crystal Palace, Debbie Bliss, Noro and Twilleys.

T: +44 (0)1665 606062

E: info@paviyarns.com

www.sheepfold.co.uk

This site includes a shop where some of the yarns used in this book can be purchased worldwide. Sheepfold also let you know the sales events that they will be attending, where the Sheepfold wool and British Breeds yarns can be seen and purchased by customers.

T: +44 (0)794 090 7738

E: sales@sheepfold.co.uk

www.texere.co.uk

This site includes a shop where some of the yarns used in this book can be purchased worldwide. These include their own brand Texere wools and those produced by Mirasol, Noro and Twilleys. They also sell Prym bag handles.

T: +44 (0)1274 722191

E: info@texereyarns.co.uk

www.wensleydalelongwool sheepshop.co.uk

Online ordering is not available, but you can order Wensleydale Longwool yarns by phone or email or by visiting their shop.

T: +44 (0)1969 623840

E: sheepshop@lineone.net

www.woolneedlework.com

This site includes a shop where some of the yarns used in this book can be purchased in North America and Canada. These include those from Cascade, Colinette, Debbie Bliss and Noro.

T: (toll-free) 1-888-408-3777

E: info@woolneedlework.com

www.yarnmarket.com

This site includes a shop where some of the yarns used in this book can be purchased worldwide. These include those from Cascade, Crystal Palace, Debbie Bliss, Noro, Sirdar and Wendy.

T: (toll-free) 1-888-996-9276

ABOUT THE AUTHORS

Alice Underwood and Sue Parker discovered a shared passion for all things crafty when they first met in 2000. Despite having learned many different crafts, they had always focused on textiles and yarn. Sharing their knowledge and experiences, they started to explore new ideas in the craft world. In 2005, after attending a knitting design course, they began designing and felting bags. The following year, while visiting Woolfest in Cumbria (England), people repeatedly asked them where they could buy the bags they were carrying. Thus a challenge presented itself: to turn their ideas into something that others could enjoy. The result is their knit and felt company, Sheepfold.

Alice is inspired by bright colours and Sue takes ideas from shapes; both are reflected in the original and unique designs for their bags. When leaving employment in the health service, Alice studied textile and fibre art at college, and Sue has been hand spinning and dyeing for many years. Both are knitters since childhood.

In the world outside crafts, both are doctors; Alice trained as a physicist and Sue is a part-time general practitioner. Sue even gets her patients involved in knitting hats for the homeless and teddies for tragedies.

This is their first book. They hope it shows what brilliant fun can be had by turning something as simple as animal hair into a unique and useful bag.

ACKNOWLEDGEMENTS

In this, our first venture into publishing, we have been supported by many people. Here, at our own award ceremony, are the thank yous:

• To our husbands, James and Stuart, for all their encouragement. Thank you for the photographs, too, James!

• To our families for their general enthusiasm and sense of humour.

• To our test knitters and pattern checkers, Sheila Rowlands, Cath Parker and Frances Haigh, not only for checking but also for helping to produce clear instructions.

• To Nick Lovick, freelance photographer, and John Lane, sheep farmer, for permitting us to use their superb photographs of North Ronaldsay sheep.

• To our crafting friends who got us into this in the first place!

• To GMC for advice and the opportunity to spread our knowledge and enthusiasm far and wide. Especially to Dominique Page who has remained calm, cheerful and helpful throughout.

• … and especially to each other for making such a good team together.

INDEX

To place an order, or to request a catalogue, contact:
GMC Publications
Castle Place, 166 High Street, Lewes, East Sussex, BN7 1XU
United Kingdom
Tel: 01273 488005 Fax: 01273 402866
Website: www.gmcbooks.com
Orders by credit card are accepted